GRADE

everyday Writing
Intervention Activities

Table of Contents

Using Everyday Writing Intervention Activities

Research shows that reading and writing are reciprocal processes, and often the same students who struggle as readers need support to develop their writing skills.

The Everyday Writing Intervention Activities provide developmentally appropriate, easy-to-use, five-day writing units for Grades K–5. Each unit focuses on a particular writing process or writer's craft skill and provides multiple opportunities for students to practice that skill. As students complete these engaging mini-lessons, they will build a repertoire of writing skills they can apply as they write independently during writer's workshop, respond to texts they have read, complete content-area writing assignments, or write to prompts on standardized assessments.

These units are structured around a research-based model-guide-practice-apply approach. You can use these activities in a variety of intervention models, including Response to Intervention (RTI).

Getting Started

In just five simple steps, Everyday Writing Intervention Activities provides everything you need to identify students' needs and to provide targeted intervention.

online

1. PRE-ASSESS to identify students'
writing needs. Use the pre-assessment to identify the skills your students need to master.

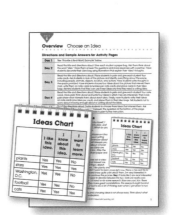

Day 1

2. MODEL the skill.
Every five-day unit targets a specific writing study area. On Day 1, use the teacher prompts and reproducible activity page to introduce and model the skill.

Day 2   **Day 3**   **Day 4**

3. GUIDE, PRACTICE, and APPLY.
Use the reproducible practice activities for Days 2, 3, and 4 to build students' understanding and skill proficiency.

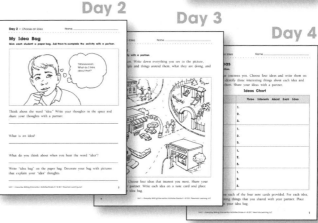

Day 5

4. MONITOR progress.
Administer the Day 5 reproducible assessment to monitor each student's progress and to make instructional decisions.

5. POST-ASSESS to document student progress.
Use the post-assessment to measure students' progress as a result of your interventions.

online

Standards-Based Writing Awareness & Writing Skills in Everyday Intervention Activities

The writing strategies found in the Everyday Intervention Activities series are introduced developmentally and spiral from one grade to the next. The chart below shows the types of words and skill areas addressed at each grade level in this series.

Everyday Writing Intervention Activities Series Skills	K	1	2	3	4	5
Choosing a topic	✔	✔	✔	✔	✔	✔
Narrow the focus	✔	✔	✔	✔	✔	✔
Develop the idea (list what I know, research, complete list)	✔	✔	✔	✔	✔	✔
Organizing ideas/Writing an outline	✔	✔	✔	✔	✔	✔
Strong leads (fiction)	✔	✔	✔	✔	✔	✔
Strong leads (nonfiction)	✔	✔	✔	✔	✔	✔
Developing a character	✔	✔	✔	✔	✔	✔
Developing a plot	✔	✔	✔	✔	✔	✔
Strong endings (fiction)	✔	✔	✔	✔	✔	✔
Strong endings (nonfiction)	✔	✔	✔	✔	✔	✔
What is voice?	✔	✔	✔	✔	✔	✔
How do I write in my voice?	✔	✔	✔	✔	✔	✔
Different voices	✔	✔	✔	✔	✔	✔
Adjectives	✔	✔	✔	✔	✔	✔
Adverbs	✔	✔	✔	✔	✔	✔
Verbs	✔	✔	✔	✔	✔	✔
Nouns	✔	✔	✔	✔		
Advanced nouns					✔	✔
Idioms			✔	✔	✔	✔
Similes			✔	✔	✔	✔
Metaphors					✔	✔
Personification						✔

Everyday Writing Intervention Activities Grade 4 • ©2011 Newmark Learning, LLC

Using Everyday Intervention for RTI

According to the National Center on Response to Intervention, RTI "integrates assessment and intervention within a multi-level prevention system to maximize student achievement and to reduce behavior problems." This model of instruction and assessment allows schools to identify at-risk students, monitor their progress, provide research-proven interventions, and "adjust the intensity and nature of those interventions depending on a student's responsiveness."

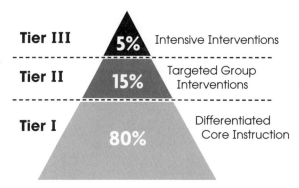

RTI models vary from district to district, but the most prevalent model is a three-tiered approach to instruction and assessment.

The Three Tiers of RTI	Using Everyday Intervention Activities
Tier I: Differentiated Core Instruction • Designed for all students • Preventive, proactive, standards-aligned instruction • Whole- and small-group differentiated instruction • Daily literacy instruction	• Use whole-group writing mini-lessons to introduce and guide practice with vocabulary strategies that all students need to learn. • Use any or all of the units in the order that supports your core instructional program.
Tier II: Targeted Group Interventions • For struggling readers and writers • Provide thirty minutes of daily instruction beyond the Tier I core literacy instruction • Instruction is conducted in small groups of three to five students with similar needs	• Select units based on your students' areas of need (the pre-assessment can help you identify these). • Use the units as week-long, small-group mini-lessons.
Tier III: Intensive Interventions • For high-risk students experiencing considerable difficulty in reading and writing • Provide up to sixty minutes of additional intensive intervention each day in addition to the ninety-minute Tier I core reading instruction • More intense and explicit instruction • Instruction conducted individually or with smaller groups of one to three students with similar needs	• Select units based on your students' areas of need. • Use the units as one component of an intensive reading and writing intervention program.

Overview Choose an Idea

Directions and Sample Answers for Activity Pages

Day 1	See "Provide a Real-World Example" below.
Day 2	Read the title and directions aloud. Give each student a paper bag. Ask them to think about the word **idea**. Have them answer the questions and share responses with a partner. Have students decorate their idea bag using illustrations that explain their **idea** thoughts.
Day 3	Read the title and directions aloud. Place students in pairs and give each student four note cards. Ask students to look at the picture and identify everything about the scene, including people, animals, objects, locations, and actions. Have students write thoughts on a separate sheet of paper. Have students choose four ideas about the picture that interest them most, write them on note cards (one idea per note card), and place cards in their idea bags. Remind students that they can use these ideas anytime they need a writing idea.
Day 4	Read the title and directions aloud. Place students in pairs and give each student four note cards. Have pairs think about and write four ideas in which they are interested. Then have pairs share what interests them about each idea. Finally, have students write their ideas on the note cards (one idea per card), and place them in their idea bags. Tell students not to worry about knowing enough about or writing about the ideas.
Day 5	Read the directions aloud. Invite students to choose three ideas that interest them. Ask students to complete the chart and answer the questions at the bottom of the page. Discuss their results. Use their responses to plan further instruction.

Provide a Real-World Example

◆ Hand out the Day 1 activity page. **Say:** *When I'm by myself, I think about different things. I think about plants, stars, and cities I would like to visit, like Washington, D.C. What do you like to think about?* Have students offer ideas.

◆ **Say:** *One of the hardest things writers do is choose an idea to write about. How do you know what is a good writing idea? There are three important things to remember about choosing a writing idea. Choose an idea that interests you. Choose an idea that you know something about. Choose an idea you want to learn more about. These ideas are important for writing both fiction and nonfiction.* After the lesson, write the three important things on chart paper and leave them hanging in the room.

Ideas Chart

	I like this idea.	I know about this idea.	I want to learn more.
plants	Yes	Yes	No
stars	Yes	Yes	Yes
Washington, D.C.	Yes	Yes	No
football	Yes	Yes	No
cats	Yes	Yes	Yes

◆ **Say:** *Look at the chart. I wrote five things that interest me, but I don't really want to write about all of them. Watch as I choose a writing idea that works for me. I like plants, and I know a little bit about them. But I really don't want to learn more right now.* Place a Yes and No in the appropriate columns. **Say:** *I love stars and know quite a bit about them. I'm very interested in constellations.* Use the completed chart to continue the process. **Say:** *It looks like I am most interested in writing about stars and cats. Now I just need to decide between the two. Cats are really cool. I could write about different kinds of cats. I'd need to do some research. Stars are cool, too. There are so many different kinds of stars, and they make great constellations. The research might be kind of fun. I think I like stars better than cats. I had to do a lot of thinking even when I got down to two ideas. Choosing an idea takes a lot of thinking.*

◆ **Say:** *Remember, all writers choose ideas, and choosing ideas is not always easy. Think about what you like and don't like before you make a decision.*

Name _____

Choose an Idea

Complete the following chart.

	I like this idea.	I know about this idea.	I want to learn more.
plants			
stars			
Washington, D.C.			
football			
cats			

Unit 1 • *Everyday Writing Intervention Activities Grade 4* • ©2011 Newmark Learning, LLC

My Idea Bag

Give each student a paper bag. Ask them to complete the activity with a partner.

Think about the word **idea**. Write your thoughts in the space and share your thoughts with a partner.

_____

What is an idea?

_____

What do you think about when you hear the word **idea**?

_____

Write "idea bag" on the paper bag. Decorate your bag with pictures that explain your **idea** thoughts.

_____

Picture This

Complete the activity with a partner.

Look at the picture. Write down everything you see in the picture, including the people and things around them, what they are doing, and where they are.

Read your ideas. Choose four ideas that interest you most. Share your choices with your partner. Write each idea on a note card and place the cards in your idea bag.

Writing Ideas

Complete the activities.

Think about what interests you. Choose four ideas and write them on the chart. Then identify three interesting things about each idea and write them on the chart. Share your ideas with a partner.

Ideas Chart

Ideas	Three Interesting Things About Each Idea
	1. 2. 3.
	1. 2. 3.
	1. 2. 3.
	1. 2. 3.

Write one idea on each of the four note cards provided. For each idea, write two interesting things that you shared with your partner. Place the note cards in your idea bag.

Assessment

Complete the activities.

Look at the chart. In the left-hand column, write three ideas that interest you. Then complete the chart with Yes or No.

Ideas Chart

Ideas	I like this idea.	I know about this idea.	I want to learn more.
1. _____			
2. _____			
3. _____			

Use the chart to answer the questions.

1. Which ideas will you not choose? Why not?

2. Which ideas might you choose? Why?

3. Look at your answer for number 2. Will you need to research these ideas before you can write?

4. Which writing idea do you choose?

Overview   Narrow the Writing Idea

Directions and Sample Answers for Activity Pages

Day 1	See "Provide a Real-World Example" below.
Day 2	Read the title and directions aloud. Invite students to read the list of foods. Then ask them to organize the list into meaningful groups and give each group a title. Ask students to think about which group they would like to write about. Ask them to share their thoughts with a partner. Remind students that there are many ways to organize the list.
Day 3	Read the title and directions aloud. Invite students to look at the pictures. Then ask students to write a list of ten things they think of when they see each picture. Remind students that there are no right or wrong answers. Students will use their ideas in the next lesson.
Day 4	Read the title and directions aloud. Have students review their lists from the previous lesson. Ask students to choose one list and organize the list into groups. Give each group a title. Have students think about which group they want to write about and share their thoughts with a partner.
Day 5	Read the directions aloud. Allow time for students to complete the tasks. Meet individually with students. Discuss their results. Use their responses to plan further instruction.

Provide a Real-World Example

◆ Hand out the Day 1 activity page. Write the word **stars** on the board. **Say:** *I've decided to write about stars. There are so many things about stars that I like. How am I going to decide what idea to write about? Watch as I choose one thing to write about. First, I'll make a list of things that have to do with stars.* Use the following ideas to generate a list of "star" ideas.

◆ **Say:** *The list is long and is not organized. I'm going to put these ideas into groups. I see that I've listed names of constellations, or groups of stars that make pictures. I'll write those in a list.* Write constellations in one list. **Say:** *I've also listed names of individual stars. I'll write those in another list.* Write individual star names in another list. **Say:** *I've listed characteristics of stars. I'll write those in a third list.* Write characteristics of stars in a third list.

Stars	Constellations	Star Names	Characteristics of Stars
Alpha Centauri	Orion	Alpha Centauri	Show light
North Star	Big Dipper	North Star	Make pictures
Show light	Little Dipper		Some are brighter than others
Make pictures	Leo		
Orion			Look like they sparkle
Big Dipper			
Little Dipper			
Some are brighter than others			
Leo			
Look like they sparkle			

◆ **Say:** *Now I need to label them so I know what the groups are about.* Review each group and label them with the following titles: "Constellations," "Star Names," and "Characteristics of Stars."

◆ **Say:** *Now I need to decide what I'm going to write about. I don't really want to write about star names or star characteristics. I think I really want to write about constellations. Organizing my ideas really helped me make a good decision.*

Narrow the Writing Idea

Write a list of everything you think of when you hear the word *stars*.

Stars

1. _____

2. _____

3. _____

4. _____

5. _____

6. _____

7. _____

8. _____

9. _____

10. _____

Group ideas into categories. Then give each group a title.

Title: _____   **Title:** _____   **Title:** _____

1. _____   1. _____   1. _____

2. _____   2. _____   2. _____

3. _____   3. _____   3. _____

4. _____   4. _____   4. _____

5. _____   5. _____   5. _____

Organize Ideas

Read the list of foods. Organize the list into groups. (Remember, there are many ways to organize ideas.)

hot dogs	mustard	relish
ketchup	fried chicken	cake
oranges	broccoli	bananas
cookies	hamburgers	
green beans	candy	

Then give each group a title. Think about each group. Which group would you like to write about most? Why? Share your thoughts with a partner.

Title: _____	**Title:** _____	**Title:** _____
1. _____	1. _____	1. _____
2. _____	2. _____	2. _____
3. _____	3. _____	3. _____
4. _____	4. _____	4. _____
5. _____	5. _____	5. _____
6. _____	6. _____	6. _____
7. _____	7. _____	7. _____

Name _____

Writing Your Ideas

Look at the pictures. For each picture, write ten things that you think about when you see the picture.

Title: _____	**Title:** _____	**Title:** _____
1. _____	1. _____	1. _____
2. _____	2. _____	2. _____
3. _____	3. _____	3. _____
4. _____	4. _____	4. _____
5. _____	5. _____	5. _____
6. _____	6. _____	6. _____
7. _____	7. _____	7. _____
8. _____	8. _____	8. _____
9. _____	9. _____	9. _____
10. _____	10. _____	10. _____

Unit 2 • *Everyday Writing Intervention Activities Grade 4* • ©2011 Newmark Learning, LLC

Narrow the Focus

Look at your lists from Day 3. Choose one list and organize the list into groups. Give each group a label. Think about each group. Which group would you like to write about? Why? Share your thoughts with a partner.

Title: _____

_____

_____

_____

_____

Title: _____

_____

_____

_____

_____

Title: _____

_____

_____

_____

_____

Title: _____

_____

_____

_____

_____

Assessment

Look at the picture. Under the picture, write ten things that you think about when you see the picture.

1. _____   5. _____   9. _____

2. _____   6. _____   10. _____

3. _____   7. _____

4. _____   8. _____

In the space below, organize the list into groups. Then give each group a title. Think about each group. Which group would you like to write about most? Why?

Title: _____   **Title:** _____   **Title:** _____

1. _____   1. _____   1. _____

2. _____   2. _____   2. _____

3. _____   3. _____   3. _____

4. _____   4. _____   4. _____

5. _____   5. _____   5. _____

Overview Develop the Writing Idea

Directions and Sample Answers for Activity Pages

Day 1	See "Provide a Real-World Example" below.
Day 2	Read the title and directions aloud. Have students read the list of ideas. Ask them to identify three things that they already know about each idea. Have students write those ideas on the lines and share their ideas with a partner.
Day 3	Read the title and directions aloud. Invite students to look at the pictures. Tell students that each picture stands for a possible writing idea. Ask students to think about each idea and identify two questions that they would like answered. Have students write their questions on the lines provided. Finally, ask students to share their questions with a partner. Remind students that each question could be used later to develop a writing idea.
Day 4	Read the title and directions aloud. Invite students to read the list of ideas. Ask students to research each idea and identify three things that they did not know about the idea. Have students write the information on the lines and share their thoughts with a partner.
Day 5	Read the directions aloud. Allow time for students to complete the task. Afterward, meet individually with students. Discuss their results. Use their responses to plan further instruction.

Provide a Real-World Example

◆ Before the lesson, draw an incomplete knowledge chart on the board. Hand out the Day 1 activity page. (See the Day 1 handout for the incomplete knowledge chart.)

◆ Write the word **constellations** on the board. **Say:** *I've decided to write about constellations. I want to include certain things, so I need to plan, or develop, my idea before I write. Asking a question helps me plan.* Write the question on the board: *What makes a constellation?* **Say:** *Answers to this question will help me plan my idea.*

◆ Draw a knowledge chart on the board. **Say:** *I'll use a knowledge chart to help me plan my idea.*

◆ Use the completed knowledge chart here to model how to develop a writing idea. **Say:** *I know people long ago looked at stars in the sky and sort of connected the dots to make pictures. I know the pictures stars make are not really clear. Constellations have names that come from Roman stories long ago. I'll write those things into the chart. Is that all I want to include in my paper? No. That doesn't seem to be enough. So what questions do I have about constellations? I don't know who came up with the constellation idea. I also don't know what the names mean. Also, can you see the same constellation in the sky every night? I'll write those questions on the chart.*

◆ Circle the last column containing the questions. **Say:** *I don't have answers to questions in the last column. I'll need to do research before I can write my paper. I can probably find information in the encyclopedia, but I like the Internet better so I'll use that.* Remind students that developing a writing idea takes time. Students should not hurry through this part of the writing process.

Knowledge Chart
Question: What makes a constellation?

What do I know?	Is this enough information?	What questions do I have?
a group of stars that makes something like a picture; the picture is not clear; they have names; the names come from Roman stories from long ago	No	Who came up with the constellation idea? What do the names mean? Can you see constellations in the same place every night?

Develop the Writing Idea

Complete the chart below.

Knowledge Chart

Question: What makes a constellation?

What do I know?	Is this enough information?	What questions do I have?

What Do You Know About It?

Read the list of ideas. For each idea, identify three things that you already know. Write your ideas on the lines and share your information with a partner.

tools

_____

_____

clothes

_____

_____

butterflies

_____

_____

cars

_____

_____

Name _____

Ask a Question ... or Two

Look at the pictures. Each picture stands for a different writing idea. Think about two questions that you have for each idea. Write your questions on the lines and share them with a partner.

bank

_____

_____

_____

paint

_____

_____

_____

farm

_____

_____

_____

grocery store

_____

_____

_____

Research It

Read the list of ideas from Day 3. Use encyclopedias or the Internet to find out three things that you did not know about each idea. Write the information on the lines and share your ideas with a partner.

bank

_____

_____

_____

paint

_____

_____

_____

farm

_____

_____

_____

grocery store

_____

_____

_____

Assessment

Read the question. Then complete the chart.

Knowledge Chart
What is soccer?

What do I know?	Is this enough information?	What questions do I have?

Overview Develop an Outline of Information

Directions and Sample Answers for Activity Pages

Day 1	See "Provide a Real-World Example" below.
Day 2	Read the title and directions aloud. Ask students to think about the words, decide what the big idea is, and write the idea on the line. Have students share their thoughts with a partner. (Possible answers: types of weather or precipitation, effects of severe weather, types of storms, tools we use to measure weather) Ask students to choose one group of words and illustrate it. Have students write and share a short paragraph explaining their illustration.
Day 3	Read the title and directions aloud. Have students look at the charts. Explain that each chart is about a different area of music. Ask students to complete each chart with three details that support each big idea. Have students share their thoughts with a partner. Then have students choose one chart and illustrate the information in it. (Possible answers: first chart—violin, trumpet, tuba; second chart—whole note, half note, quarter note; third chart—jazz, classical, country; fourth chart—"Old MacDonald," "Somewhere Over the Rainbow," "Yankee Doodle")
Day 4	Read the title and directions aloud. Have pairs of students look at the blank chart about toys. Ask students to fill in the missing information. (Possible answers: toys for babies—blocks, stuffed animals, rolling toys; toys for kids—video games, fingerpaints, clay; toys for adults—boats, jet skis, cars) Have students identify their favorite toy, draw a picture of it, and explain their answer to a partner.
Day 5	Read the directions aloud. Allow time for students to complete each task. (Possible answers: where fish live—oceans, rivers, ponds; what they eat—other fish, krill, plants; name three fish—tuna, snapper, perch; how to catch fish—with a net, with a spear, with a fishing pole) Afterward, meet individually with students to discuss their results and plan further instruction.

Provide a Real-World Example

◆ Hand out the Day 1 activity page. **Say:** *Now we are going to learn how to organize. What does the word* **organize** *mean?* (Allow responses.) **Say:** *Organize means to put things in an order that makes sense. When authors write nonfiction, they organize information in a way that makes sense. First they write down big ideas. Then they write details that support the big ideas. We call this plan an outline. I want to write a short paper about constellations. Watch as I organize my information into a chart.*

◆ **Say:** *The first thing I need to do is write down my big ideas. I need to define constellation. Next, I'll write about a few different constellations. For this paper, I may include drawings of the constellations I chose. Finally, I'll include information about each constellation, like the meaning of its name, the brightest star in the constellation, and maybe one other interesting fact. Now I'll fill in the details for each big idea.* Complete the chart.

◆ **Say:** *I wrote a lot. My next step is to write these ideas into complete sentences and work on my hook and ending. Remember to plan before you write. It makes writing easier.*

Constellations

Big Idea	Details
define constellation	a group of stars that has been given a name and makes a picture
three different constellations	Orion, Ursa Major, Leo
information about each constellation	Orion—means the Hunter, brightest star is Rigel, part of the Winter Triangle
	Ursa Major—means Greater Bear, brightest star is Alioth, it is also called the Big Dipper
	Leo—means Lion, brightest star is Regulus, it is a part of the Zodiac calendar

Develop an Outline of Information

Complete the chart.

1. Choose an idea—stars

2. Narrow an idea—constellations

3. Develop an idea—what I know and don't know about constellations

4. Develop an outline—organize information to write

Constellations

Big Idea	Details

What's the Big Idea?

Look at each group of words. Each group supports a big idea about weather. Decide what the big idea is and write it on the lines. Share your big ideas with a partner. Explain how you got your answers.

rain

hail

snow

sleet

Big Idea:

_____

_____

---

power outages

water in houses

knocked-down trees

car wrecks

Big Idea:

_____

_____

---

hurricanes

tsunamis

blizzards

tornadoes

Big Idea:

_____

_____

---

barometer

thermometer

rain gauge

weather vane

Big Idea:

_____

_____

Choose one group of words. Draw a picture that stands for the words in the group. Write a short paragraph explaining your picture. Share your paragraph and drawing with a partner.

Support the Big Idea

Look at the charts. Each chart tells something different about music. Three boxes are under each big idea. In each box, write one detail that supports its big idea. Share your thoughts with a partner.

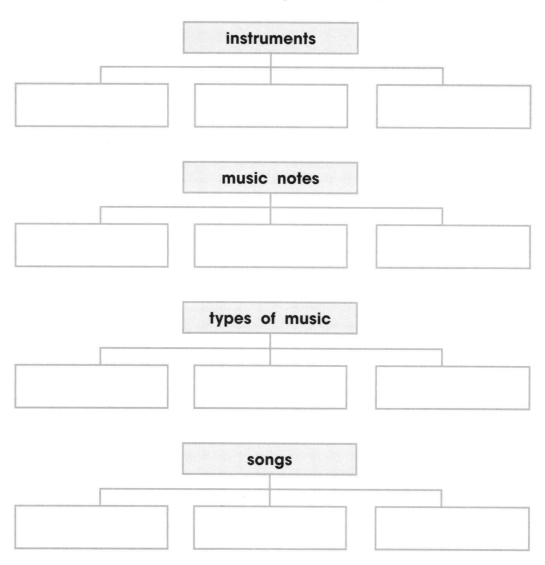

Choose one chart. Draw pictures that explain each detail.

Unit 4 • Everyday Writing Intervention Activities Grade 4 • ©2011 Newmark Learning, LLC

Make an Outline

Look at the blank chart about toys. Fill in the missing information.

Toys for All

Big Ideas	Details

What is your favorite toy? Draw a picture of it and explain your answer to your partner.

Assessment

Look at the blank chart about fish. Fill in the missing information.

Fish

Big Ideas	Details

Identify one more big idea for this chart and the details that support it.

Unit 4 • Everyday Writing Intervention Activities Grade 4 • ©2011 Newmark Learning, LLC

Overview   Strong Nonfiction Leads

Directions and Sample Answers for Activity Pages

Day 1	See "Provide a Real-World Example" below.
Day 2	Read the title and directions aloud. Ask students to analyze the leads on the chart and identify which lead they prefer. Have students share their thoughts with a partner.
Day 3	Read the title and directions aloud. Ask students to look at the pictures on the right side of the page, match each picture with its correct lead, and share their results with a partner. (Answers: **1.** house; **2.** robot; **3.** jellyfish; **4.** litter on beach; **5.** mountain) Then ask students to choose one picture and write a different lead for it. Have students share their new lead with a partner. For an extra lesson, help students analyze the different types of leads used in this exercise. (**1.** describing a sound; **2.** dialogue; **3.** using a question; **4.** stating an opinion; **5.** stating an opinion)
Day 4	Read the title and directions aloud. Ask students to write a strong lead for each picture. If students struggle, have them review leads from Day 3 and offer assistance. Ask students to share their results with a partner. Have students choose one picture and write a different lead for it. Then have students ask a partner to decide which picture matches the lead.
Day 5	Read the directions aloud. Allow time for students to complete the tasks. Afterward, meet individually with students. Discuss their results. Use their responses to plan further instruction.

Provide a Real-World Example

◆ Hand out the Day 1 activity page. Write the following nonfiction leads on the board:

Pizza is a great food.

What type of food has ooey, gooey cheese, crispy crust, and tangy tomato sauce?

◆ **Say:** *When authors write nonfiction, they begin with a sentence or two that makes readers want to keep reading. We call these sentences strong leads, or hooks.*

◆ **Say:** *Let's say that I'm going to write about one of my favorite foods, pizza. I've written two leads and can't decide which one to choose. Look at the leads on the board.*

◆ Have a student read the leads and help students analyze them and complete the chart using the following information: 1st lead—1. simply states what the author is writing about; 2. doesn't offer any information about pizza; 3. weak lead; 2nd lead—1. is written in question form; 2. offers catchy information about pizza; 3. strong lead

◆ **Ask:** *Which lead makes you want to read my paper? Why?* Allow time for student responses.

◆ **Say:** *The second lead sounds more interesting than the first. I think my readers will want to read more about pizza. Remember to use a strong lead to hook your reader.* Remind students that leads like "This paper is about . . ." or "I'm going to tell you about a . . ." are not strong leads.

Nonfiction Leads

Pizza is a great food.	What type of food has ooey, gooey cheese, crispy crust, and tangy tomato sauce?
simply states what the author is writing about; doesn't offer any information about pizza; weak lead	is written in question form; offers catchy information about pizza; strong lead

Name _____

Strong Nonfiction Leads

Complete the chart.

Nonfiction Leads

Pizza is a great food.	What type of food has ooey, gooey cheese, crispy crust, and tangy tomato sauce?

Strong and Weak Nonfiction Leads

Read the nonfiction leads. Tell which lead is strong and which lead is weak. Explain your thoughts on the chart. Answer the question at the bottom of the page and share your thoughts with a partner.

Sand Castles

I'm going to tell you about sand castles.	Sand castles. The word makes you think of salty air, gritty sand between your toes, and lots of digging.

Which lead do you like better? Why?

_____

Lead Match-Up

Look at the pictures on the right side of the page. Each picture represents a nonfiction writing idea. Read the strong nonfiction leads on the left side of the page. Draw a line from the picture to its matching lead. Share your results with a partner.

Strong Nonfiction Leads

1. *Creak. Creak. Creak.* There is nothing like an old house to really get you in a spooky mood.

2. "Wow!" the boy exclaimed. "That robot can do everything a human can do."

3. Have you ever seen anything as funny looking as a jellyfish? The name really suits the animal.

4. I think people should try hard to pick up trash wherever they are.

5. Snow-covered mountains are beautiful to look at, but they are also great fun to climb up and ski down.

Pictures

Choose one picture and write a different lead for it. Share your lead with a partner.

Write a Lead

Look at the pictures. Each picture stands for a nonfiction writing idea. Write a strong nonfiction lead for each picture and share your leads with a partner. Then choose one picture and write a different lead for it. Ask a partner to decide which picture matches the lead.

Assessment

Read the nonfiction leads. Tell which lead is strong and which lead is weak.
Explain what makes each lead strong or weak.

Lollipops

Lollipops are the best candy.	Lollipops. Crunchy lollipops. Sticky lollipops. There has never been a candy more perfect than lollipops.

Look at the picture and write a strong nonfiction lead.

broccoli

_____

_____

Overview   Strong Nonfiction Endings

Directions and Sample Answers for Activity Pages

Day 1	See "Provide a Real-World Example" below.
Day 2	Read the title and directions aloud. Ask students to analyze the endings on the chart and identify which ending they prefer. Have students share their thoughts with a partner.
Day 3	Read the title and directions aloud. Ask students to match each picture on the right side of the page with its correct ending. Have students share their results with a partner. (Answers: **1.** Abraham Lincoln; **2.** sun; **3.** bird; **4.** blueprint; **5.** full recycling bin) Ask students to choose one picture and write a different ending for it. Have students share their new ending with a partner. For an extra lesson, help students analyze the different types of endings used in this exercise. (**1.** and **2.** restate an important idea; **3.** summarize information; **4.** call to action; **5.** change way of thinking)
Day 4	Read the title and directions aloud. Ask students to write a strong ending for each picture. Have them review endings from Day 3 and offer assistance. Ask students to share their results with a partner. Have students choose one picture and write a different ending for it. Have students ask a partner to decide which picture matches the ending.
Day 5	Read the directions aloud. Allow time for students to complete the tasks. Afterward, meet individually with students. Discuss their results. Use their responses to plan further instruction.

Provide a Real-World Example

◆ Hand out the Day 1 activity page. Write the following nonfiction endings on the board:

Polar bears make nature fun.

Polar bears attack and defend, but mostly they just want to live. They are truly amazing animals.

◆ **Say:** *When authors write nonfiction, they begin with a strong lead that makes readers want to keep reading. Writers also want to end with sentences that keep their readers thinking. Let's say that I'm going to write about polar bears. I've written two endings and can't decide which one to choose. Look at the endings on the board.* Have one student read the endings and help students analyze them and complete the chart using the information in the chart on the right.

◆ **Ask:** *Which ending makes you think about how amazing polar bears really are? Why?* Allow time for student responses. **Say:** *The second ending sounds more interesting than the first. I think my readers will think about polar bears because I added some of the things they do. I sort of summarized their actions. Remember to use a strong ending to help your readers think.* Remind students that endings like "This paper was about . . ." or "These _____ are wonderful." are not strong endings.

Nonfiction Endings

Polar bears make nature fun.	Polar bears attack and defend, but mostly they just want to live. They are truly amazing animals.
simply states what the author is writing about; doesn't offer any information about polar bears; weak ending	summarizes what is so amazing about polar bears; offers information about polar bears; strong ending

Strong Nonfiction Endings

Complete the chart.

Nonfiction Endings

Polar bears make nature fun.	Polar bears attack and defend, but mostly they just want to live. They are truly amazing animals.

Strong and Weak Nonfiction Endings

Read the nonfiction endings. Tell which ending is strong and which ending is weak. Explain your thoughts. Answer the question at the bottom of the page and share your thoughts with a partner.

Lions

Lions are the most dangerous animals on the African plain.	Lions have sharp claws, sharp teeth, a huge body, and a huge tail. What animal wouldn't be afraid?

Which ending do you like better? Why?

_____

_____

Ending Match-Up

Look at the pictures on the right side of the page. Each picture stands for a nonfiction writing idea. Read the nonfiction endings on the left side of the page. Draw a line from the picture to its matching ending. Share your results with a partner.

Strong Nonfiction Endings

Pictures

1. Abraham Lincoln was a great man because he could make hard decisions and get people to follow him.

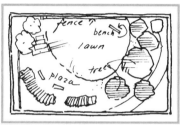

2. The sun. An object thousands of miles away, yet it still makes us wonder. Now that's amazing.

3. Birds come in all sizes and colors. They have beautiful songs that warm our hearts. What a gift from nature.

4. The fine people of this community have the power to build a wonderful park for our children. Stand with me today on this issue.

5. Recycling may take some time and a little bit of money, but what would happen to Earth if we didn't recycle?

Choose one picture and write a different lead for it. Share your lead with a partner.

Write an Ending

Look at the pictures. Each picture stands for a nonfiction writing idea. Write a strong nonfiction ending for each picture and share your endings with a partner.

_____

_____

_____

_____

_____

_____

_____

_____

_____

Choose one picture and write a different ending for it. Ask a partner to decide which picture matches the ending.

Assessment

Read the nonfiction endings. Tell which ending is strong and
which ending is weak. Explain what makes each ending strong or weak.

Baseball

I think kids should be able to play baseball.	All kids should have the chance to play baseball. Won't you help us rebuild our field?

Look at the picture and write a strong nonfiction ending.

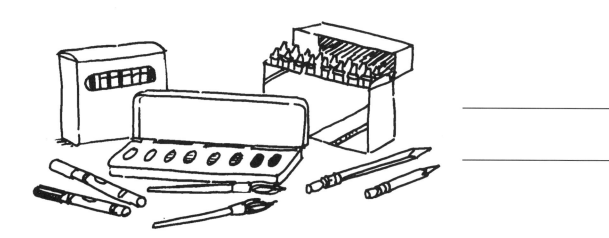

_____

_____

Overview Develop a Plot

Directions and Sample Answers for Activity Pages

Day 1	See "Provide a Real-World Example" below.
Day 2	Read the title and directions aloud. Have students think of a story idea that they might like to write about. Where does the story take place? What does the setting look like? Then ask students to draw the setting. Finally, have students share their drawings with a partner.
Day 3	Read the title and directions aloud. Ask students to complete the stories by drawing the missing events. Finally, have students share their drawings with a partner.
Day 4	Read the title and directions aloud. Have students read the story events and order the events from 1 to 8. Have students share their thoughts with a partner. Then have students choose one event and illustrate it. Have students ask a partner to identify which event was illustrated. (Answers: **1.** Walter loved flying . . . ; **2.** Even though he knew better . . . ; **3.** Walter was high in the sky . . . ; **4.** a big gust of wind . . . ; **5.** "This is not good," . . . ; **6.** Just then, a forest ranger . . . ; **7.** After about an hour, . . . ; **8.** "I think my flying days are over," . . .)
Day 5	Read the directions aloud. Allow time for students to complete the tasks. Afterward, meet individually with students. Discuss their results. Use their responses to plan further instruction.

Provide a Real-World Example

◆ Hand out the Day 1 activity page. Write the word **plot** on the board. **Ask:** *What makes a story interesting to you?* Allow responses. **Say:** *The things, or events, that happen in a story are called the plot. Good authors spend time planning, or developing, a plot before they start writing. To develop a plot, authors make decisions about time, setting, characters, and the big events that will occur in their story. Watch as I develop the plot for the story.*

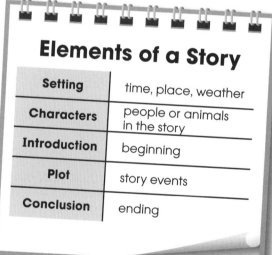

Elements of a Story

Setting	time, place, weather
Characters	people or animals in the story
Introduction	beginning
Plot	story events
Conclusion	ending

◆ Use the information in the chart to show students how to develop the time, place, and introduction to a spooky short story. **Say:** *First I need to decide on my setting, which is time and place. I think the time should be in the present during the dead of winter. It is early morning and the sun is rising. I'll choose a forest with a lake. Mist rises from the lake like steam. I'll also include the weather. It's cold, but not freezing. The beginning, or introduction, of my story will be about a brother and sister on their way to school. Now I'll develop the plot for the rest of the story.*

◆ Use the chart to show students how to develop the rest of the plot for the spooky short story. Explain that each event connects to the next event and the problem pushes the story. Point out that the first event is the problem. What are the kids going to do? The remaining events answer the question. Point out that the fifth event is the resolution to the problem. The kids find out what caused their problem. **Say:** *The last thing I need to do is decide how my story will end. This is called the conclusion. I think the brother and sister have a great story to tell their friends at school. They also decide that they won't walk that way again . . . or will they? Let me write in my conclusion.* Help students analyze the story's conclusion. Point out the ellipsis and the words "or will they" indicating that the kids may change their mind. This writing technique leaves a lot to the reader's imagination.

◆ **Say:** *Remember that this chart just shows my big events and ideas. To write a really good short story, I need to include details about the setting and characters. All of these things will keep my readers interested and maybe a little scared.*

Develop a Plot

Complete the plot chart.

Plot Chart

Time	
Place	
Introduction	
Plot (Story Events)	
Conclusion	

Unit 7 • Everyday Writing Intervention Activities Grade 4 • ©2011 Newmark Learning, LLC

Draw a Setting

Think of a story idea that you might like to write about. Where does your story take place? What does the setting look like? In the space below, use crayons, pencils, and/or markers to draw your setting. Remember, the more details you include, the better your drawing and writing will be.

What Happened?

Read the stories. In each story, two events are missing.
Draw the missing events in the boxes. Share your drawings with a partner.

Story #1

First event

It was a gorgeous day. Robin was ready to plant her apple seeds. She went to the garage and gathered all the materials she would need. Then she headed to the backyard.

Second event

Third event

Fourth event

"Ahhhh!" yelled Robin. "That bird just ate my apple seeds. Oh, brother. I hope it tasted good."

Story #2

First event

Tommy hit the baseball as hard as he could and ran. He made it to second base. He hoped that Alan would get a good hit so he could run home.

Second event

Third event

Fourth event

"You're safe!" the umpire yelled. "Yes!" Tommy said to himself. "Now I need to go thank Alan for getting a great hit."

Plot Order

The story below is about Walter and his hot air balloon. Read the story events. They are out of order. Order the events from 1 to 8. Share your thoughts with a partner.

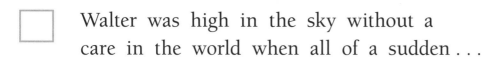

☐ "This is not good," Walter said. "What am I going to do now?"

☐ Even though he knew better, Walter decided to go flying on a windy day.

☐ Just then, a forest ranger yelled, "Hey you, stay right there. Firefighters are on their way."

☐ Walter was high in the sky without a care in the world when all of a sudden . . .

☐ "I think my flying days are over," Walter said in a shaky voice.

☐ Walter loved flying hot air balloons.

☐ a big gust of wind pushed Walter's balloon right into a group of very tall pine trees.

☐ After about an hour, the firefighters got Walter out of the tree.

Choose one event and draw a picture of it in the space. Ask a partner to decide which event you drew.

Assessment

Read the plot chart. Some information is missing. Complete the chart.

Plot Chart

Time	Place	Introduction	Story Events (Plot)	Conclusion
nine in the morning on a bright summer day	the family car, driving through the mountains	John and James, the twins, are on vacation with their parents.	a bear walks in front of the car	

Read the story events below. Two events are missing.
Draw the missing events in the boxes provided.

First event Michael and Jack are playing in the pool.

Second event	*Third event*

Fourth event

Cassie, the family dog, stands by the pool and shakes off water.

Overview Develop a Character

Directions and Sample Answers for Activity Pages

Day 1	See "Provide a Real-World Example" below.
Day 2	Read the title and directions aloud. Have students share their drawings with a partner.
Day 3	Read the title and directions aloud. Have students look at the two sets of character pictures. Ask them what they think might have happened to change the character. Then ask them to write their ideas on the lines between the two pictures. Have students share their thoughts with a partner.
Day 4	Read the title and directions aloud. Have students look at the character webs. To the side of each web, ask students to draw pictures of how Cindy changes over time. Have students share their drawings with a partner.
Day 5	Read the directions aloud. Allow time for students to complete the task. Afterward, meet individually with students. Discuss their results. Use their responses to plan further instruction.

Provide a Real-World Example

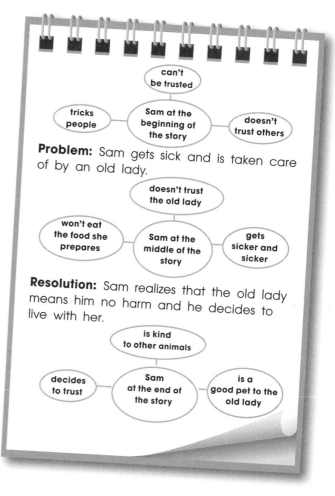

◆ Hand out the Day 1 activity page. **Say:** *Characters are the most important part of a story. Good writers make a plan for each character before they start writing. They decide what characters will look like and how they will act. These are called character traits. Then as the story develops, so do the characters. They may keep the same traits or change traits because of story events.*

◆ **Say:** *This is a character chart for Sam. He's in a story I want to write. Sam is an interesting character because he's a fox. He has the qualities we think of when we talk about foxes: he tricks people, he likes to have his own way, and he can't be trusted. When I write my story about Sam, I'll be sure to include details that support Sam's character traits.*

◆ Complete the first character web. **Say:** *I want my story to be interesting, so I need something to happen. I need a problem. Maybe my problem is that Sam gets sick one day and is found by an old lady. Now I need to decide how I'm going to develop Sam's character from this event. Help me change Sam in the second character web.* Help students revise Sam in the second character web to match the problem.

◆ **Say:** *I need to keep my story moving, so I need the problem to be resolved. Maybe Sam finally realizes the old lady means him no harm. She finally gets him to eat some food. Maybe he decides that he wants to live with the old lady. Let's change Sam one more time to match that event.* Help students revise Sam to match the resolution.

◆ **Say:** *That took some thinking. We must remember that a character's actions match what is happening in the story. For a character to develop, the author keeps both character and story events in mind when writing.*

Develop a Character

Complete the character webs.

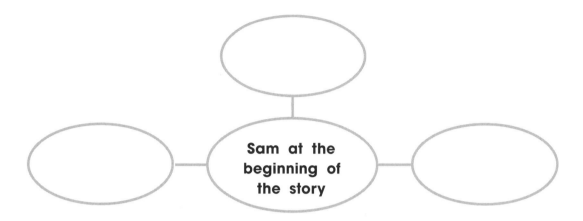

Problem: Sam gets sick and is taken care of by an old lady.

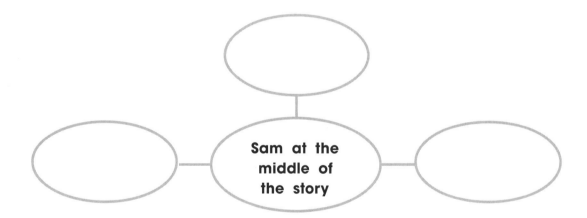

Resolution: Sam realizes that the old lady means him no harm and he decides to live with her.

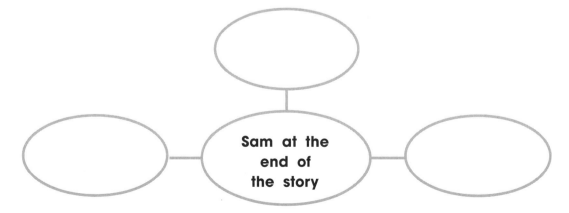

Characters Change . . . But Why?

Look at the pictures and read the sentences. Draw how you think the problem might affect the character. Share your drawings with a partner.

Problem: A girl pushes the boy away and begins to drink from the water fountain. How is the boy affected by the girl's actions?

Problem: The little boy throws a block at his mother. How is the little boy affected by his actions?

Problem: The man lifts his head up and bangs his head on the hood of the car. How is the man affected by his actions?

What Happened?

Look at the two sets of character pictures. What do you think might have happened to change the character? Write your ideas in between the pictures. Share your thoughts with a partner.

Develop a Character

Look at the character webs. They tell how a character named
Cindy changes in a story. Think about how each web describes Cindy.
For each web, draw pictures that show what you think Cindy looks like.
Share your thoughts with a partner.

Problem: Cindy is asked to be in a dance
recital, but she's so scared she doesn't know if
she can do it.

Resolution: Cindy performs on stage with the
other girls. The dance recital is a hit.

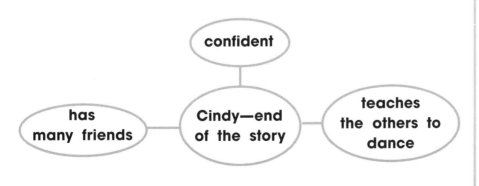

Assessment

Read the first character web. Use it to develop the same character in the other character webs.

Problem: Anna's mother makes her take swimming lessons.

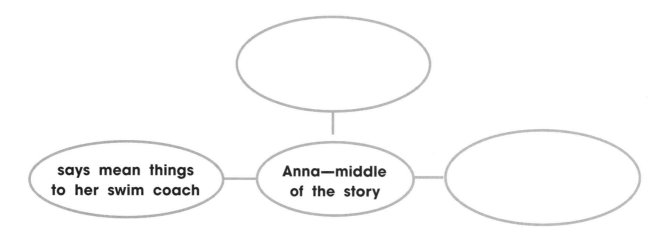

Resolution: Anna learns to swim and enjoys it.

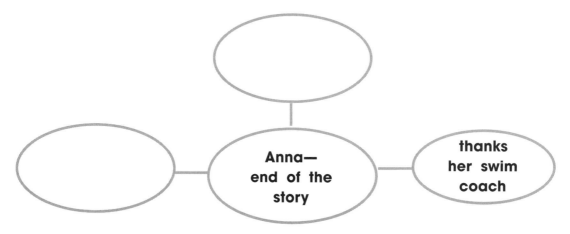

Overview   Strong Fiction Leads

Directions and Sample Answers for Activity Pages

Day 1	See "Provide a Real-World Example" below.
Day 2	Read the title and directions aloud. Ask students to analyze the leads and identify which lead they prefer. Have students share their thoughts with a partner.
Day 3	Read the title and directions aloud. Ask students to match each picture on the right side of the page with its correct lead. Ask students to share their results with a partner. (Answers: **1.** child's messy bedroom; **2.** garden in spring; **3.** elephants; **4.** library; **5.** little boy with pet turtle) Finally, ask students to choose one picture and write a different lead for it. Have students share their new lead with a partner. For an extra lesson, help students analyze the different types of leads used in this exercise. (**1.** question; **2.** opinion; **3.** dialogue; **4.** describing a sound; **5.** opinion)
Day 4	Read the title and directions aloud. Ask students to write a strong lead for each picture. If students struggle, have them review leads from Day 3 and offer assistance. Ask students to share their results with a partner. Have students choose one picture and write a different lead for it. Then have students ask a partner to decide which picture matches the lead.
Day 5	Read the directions aloud. Allow time for students to complete the tasks. Afterward, meet individually with students. Discuss their results. Use their responses to plan further instruction.

Provide a Real-World Example

◆ Hand out the Day 1 activity page. Write the following fiction leads on the board:

This story is about two kids on summer vacation.

Rain. Rain. And more rain. You wouldn't think a summer vacation filled with rain would be good, but thanks to rain, we had a great time.

◆ **Say:** *When authors write stories, they begin with a sentence or two that make readers want to keep reading. These sentences are strong leads, or hooks. Let's say that I'm going to write a story about a summer vacation. I've written two leads and can't decide which one to choose. Look at the leads on the board.* Have a student read the leads and help students analyze them by completing the chart. Use the information on the right.

◆ **Ask:** *Which lead makes you want to read my story? Why?* Allow time for student responses. **Say:** *The second lead sounds more interesting than the first. I think my readers will want to find out what happened during the vacation. Remember to use a strong lead that hooks readers.*

◆ Remind students that leads like "This story is about . . ." or "I'm going to tell you a story about a . . ." are not strong leads.

Fiction Leads

This story is about two kids on summer vacation.	Rain. Rain. And more rain. You wouldn't think a summer vacation filled with rain would be good, but thanks to the rain, we had a great time.
simply states what the author is writing about; doesn't offer any information about the vacation; weak lead	begins with one word—very catchy; the beginning word makes the reader think the vacation would be bad because no one wants rain during vacation, yet the rest of the lead lets the reader know that the vacation was actually good—how can that be?; strong lead

Strong Fiction Leads

Complete the chart.

Fiction Leads

This story is about two kids on summer vacation.	Rain. Rain. And more rain. You wouldn't think a summer vacation filled with rain would be good, but thanks to the rain, we had a great time.

Name _____

Strong and Weak Fiction Leads

Read the story leads. Tell which lead is strong and which lead is weak. Explain your thoughts in the space provided. Answer the question at the bottom of the page and share your thoughts with a partner.

Rodney

I'm going to tell you a story about a dog named Rodney.	Rodney. What a great dog. Could any person be a better friend?

Which lead do you like better? Why?

_____

Fiction Lead Match-Up

Look at the pictures on the right side of the page. Each picture represents a story. Read the strong fiction leads on the left side of the page. Draw a line from the picture to its matching lead. Share your thoughts with a partner.

Strong Fiction Leads

Pictures

1. What a mess. What a MESS! How could one little boy destroy a room in only ten minutes?

2. Ahhhh. Spring again. Nothing feels so good as warm dirt between your toes. What should I do first?

3. "Come on, Mom!" I shouted. "Do I have to perform at the circus tonight? All the other elephant kids are going to the movies."

4. *Whirr. Whirr. Whirr.* The library was kind of spooky. What could that sound be?

5. The turtle was not soft, but she was so pretty. And she seemed to want to be my friend. I guess it's a she.

Choose one picture and write a different lead for it. Share your lead with a partner.

Write a Lead

Look at the pictures. Each picture stands for a story. Write a strong story lead for each picture and share your leads with a partner.

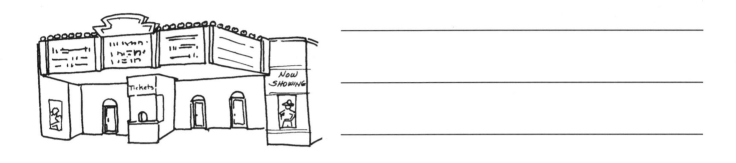

_____

_____

_____

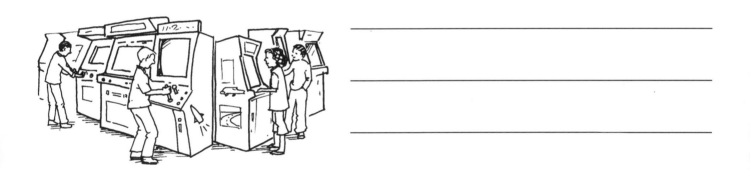

_____

_____

_____

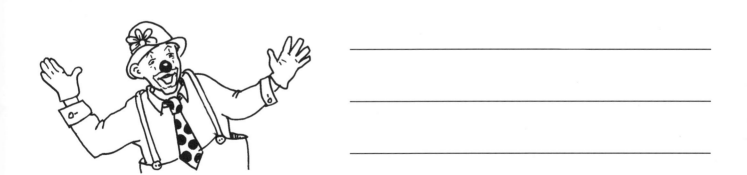

_____

_____

_____

Choose one picture and write a different lead for it. Ask a partner to decide which picture matches the lead.

Name _____

Assessment

Read the following story leads. Tell which lead is strong and which lead is weak. Explain what makes each lead strong or weak.

Lollipops in Bed?

I went to bed with a lollipop in my mouth.	This is a disaster! Why didn't I listen to my mother?

Look at the picture from a story. Write a strong lead for the story.

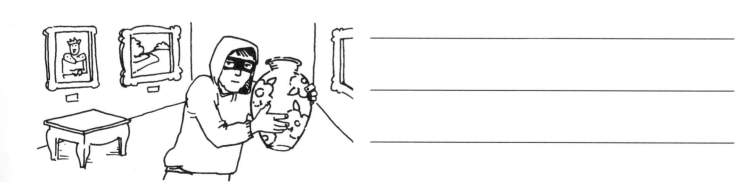

_____

_____

_____

Overview Strong Fiction Endings

Directions and Sample Answers for Activity Pages

Day 1	See "Provide a Real-World Example" below.
Day 2	Read the title and directions aloud. Invite students to look at the chart and read the endings. Then ask students to analyze the endings and identify which ending they prefer. Finally, have students share their thoughts with a partner.
Day 3	Read the title and directions aloud. Invite students to match the pictures on the right side of the page with its correct ending. Ask students to share their results with a partner. (Answers: **1.** flat tire; **2.** science fair; **3.** first place; **4.** calm volcano; **5.** two fish) Finally, ask students to choose one picture and write a different ending for it. Have students share their new ending with a partner. For an extra lesson, help students analyze the different types of endings used in this exercise. (**1.** restating an important idea in the story; **2.** life goes on; **3.** personal observation; **4.** looking toward the future; **5.** humor)
Day 4	Read the title and directions aloud. Ask students to write a strong ending for each picture. If students struggle, have them review endings from Day 3. Ask students to share their results with a partner. Have students choose one picture and write a different ending for it. Then have students ask a partner to decide which picture matches the ending.
Day 5	Read the directions aloud. Allow time for students to complete the tasks. Afterward, meet individually with students. Discuss their results. Use their responses to plan further instruction.

Provide a Real-World Example

◆ Hand out the Day 1 activity page. Write the following fiction leads on the board:

This is the end of my story.

Good grief. I was glad today was over. Tomorrow had to be a better day.

◆ **Say:** *When authors write stories, they begin with a strong lead that makes readers want to keep reading. Writers also want to end with sentences that keep their readers thinking. Let's say that I have written a story about a boy and his terrible day. One thing after another went wrong. I've written two endings and can't decide which one to choose. Look at the endings on the board.*

◆ Have one student read the endings and help students analyze them and complete the chart as shown.

◆ **Ask:** *Which ending makes you think? Why?* Allow time for student responses. **Say:** *The second ending sounds more interesting than the first. The second ending reminds me of what happened to the boy. It also helps me remember that tomorrow is always another day. Just because bad things happen on one day does not mean that good things can't happen the next day.*

◆ Remind students that endings like "My story is done." or "This is the end of my story." are not strong endings.

Fiction Endings

This is the end of my story.	Good grief. I was glad today was over. Tomorrow had to be a better day.
simply states that the author has finished writing the story; doesn't leave the reader thinking; weak ending	tells that there is hope for tomorrow; might make readers remember when they've had a bad day; strong ending

Strong Fiction Endings

Complete the chart.

Fiction Endings

This is the end of my story.	Good grief. I was glad today was over. Tomorrow had to be a better day.

Strong and Weak Fiction Endings

These endings complete a story about a dog who likes to chase chickens. Read the endings. Tell which ending is strong and which ending is weak. Explain your thoughts on the chart. Answer the question at the bottom of the page and share your thoughts with a partner.

I Love Chickens

I can't wait to chase chickens again tomorrow.	So I got into a little bit of trouble. So I got pecked at a little bit. It was a wonderful day full of chickens.

Which ending do you like better? Why?

_____

Name _____

Story Ending Match-Up

Look at the pictures on the right side of the page. Each picture represents a story. Read the strong endings on the right side of the page. Draw a line from the picture to its matching ending. Share your results with a partner.

Strong Fiction Endings

Pictures

1. It's true. The whole world is our neighbor.

2. I'd done all I could do. I'd just have to wait until tomorrow and see if my science fair project got a good grade.

3. "Winning isn't everything," Johnny thought to himself. "But it sure is nice when it happens."

4. The volcano was quiet now. But who knew for how long? The village had to prepare for the next eruption or it would be destroyed.

5. "I told you to stay away from hooks," Tommy Tuna said. "But you talk so much, I never know when to believe you," replied Tammy Tuna.

Choose one picture and write a different ending for it. Share your ending with a partner.

Name _____

Write an Ending

Look at the pictures. Each picture stands for a story.
Write a strong ending for each picture and share them with a partner.

_____

_____

_____

_____

_____

_____

**Choose one picture and write a different ending for it.
Ask a partner to decide which picture matches the ending.**

Assessment

Read the story endings. Tell which ending is strong and which
ending is weak. Explain what makes each ending strong or weak.

The Museum

The museum was really great.	Who would have thought a museum could be such fun?

Look at the picture from a story. Write a strong ending for the story.

_____

_____

_____

Overview   Using Voice

Directions and Sample Answers for Activity Pages

Day 1	See "Provide a Real-World Example" below.
Day 2	Read the title and directions aloud. Ask students to choose a partner and act out what the objects might say to each other. Remind students to use voice. Have each student choose one scene and write the conversation on the lines.
Day 3	Read the title and directions aloud. Have students choose a partner and read each sentence. Ask pairs to decide how the sentences might be said to their mother and to their friend. Have partners act out the sentences. Finally, have students choose one sentence and write it down the way they would say it to their mother and to their friend.
Day 4	Read the title and directions aloud. Have students read the sentences in the left column. Ask students to read the words in the right column. Ask them to think about who the audience for each sentence might be. Have students draw a line matching the sentence on the left with its corresponding audience on the right. Have students share their results with a partner. Then have students choose one sentence and illustrate it.
Day 5	Read the directions aloud. Allow time for students to complete the task. (Possible answers: **1.** Mom—Mom, I finished folding the clothes.; Friend—Okay. I finally finished the clothes. Now we can go.; **2.** Principal—I promise to never write in the textbook again.; Friend—Man, did I get in trouble. I'll never write in textbooks again.; **3.** Dog—Okay. Your food is in the bowl so eat up.; Sick parent—Your food's ready, so can I bring it to you on a tray?; **4.** Neighbor—May I borrow a cup of sugar?; Little sister—Bring me the sugar. I need a cup.) Meet individually with students. Discuss their results. Use their responses to plan further instruction.

Provide a Real-World Example

◆ Hand out the Day 1 activity page. **Ask:** *When we write, we want our words to sound like the way we would really speak. This is called voice. Think about how you would ask your mom for five dollars. Now think about how you might ask your best friend for five dollars.*

◆ Have a student read both notes. **Say:** *The note to my mom and the note to Debra say the same thing, but they sound very different. Let's analyze them.* Use the information in the chart at right to help students analyze the differences between the two notes.

◆ **Say:** *These notes are written for different kinds of people so they should sound different. This is an example of using different voices for different audiences. What is an audience?* Allow time for student responses. **Say:** *An audience is someone who is watching you perform. An audience might watch you perform in a dance recital, a karate match, a soccer game, or a play. An audience is also the person who reads what you write. Writing audiences can be a friend, a principal, a parent or grandparent, a teacher, or even the President of the United States. Remember your audience when you write so that you will use the right voice.*

Different Voices

Mom, I want five dollars.	Mom, I know you are really busy right now, but I was wondering if I could have five dollars. I found a book that I would like to have at the book fair. What do you say?
tells Mom you need money	tells Mom that you know she's busy; you ask for money in a nice way (wondering); tell why you need the money

Name _____

Using Voice

Analyze the differences between the notes below. Complete the chart.

Different Voices for Different Audiences

Mom, I know you are really busy right now, but I was wondering if I could have five dollars. I found a book that I would like to have at the book fair. What do you say?	Debra, can I borrow five dollars? I'll pay you back tomorrow.

Using Voice

Read the scenes. With your partner, act out a short conversation that might happen between the two objects. Remember that each object has a voice.

french fries and ketchup

a candle and a match

a patio and acorns falling from a nearby tree

a golf ball and a golf club

Choose one scene and write the conversation on the lines.

_____

_____

_____

_____

_____

_____

Voice Choice

Read the sentence.

Don't feed your broccoli to the dog.

Who might say this sentence? A sister, a mother, a friend? Each person would say that sentence in a different voice and using different words.

A sister might use a bratty voice and say, "Mom, Johnny's feeding his broccoli to the dog again." A mother might use a firm voice and say, "Johnny. Do not feed your broccoli to that dog." A friend might use a hurried, whispered voice and say, "Johnny, are you nuts? Your mom's going to get mad if she finds out you fed your broccoli to the dog."

Read each sentence. Decide how you would rephrase the sentence and say it to your mother and to your friend. Then act out the sentence with your partner.

1. I can't believe you just did that.

2. I think I can climb out on the roof and get the ball down.

3. I need to give the dog a bath.

4. Why do people have to be so mean?

Choose one sentence. Write how you would say the sentence to your mom. Then write how you would say the sentence to your friend.

_____

_____

_____

_____

Who's the Audience?

Read the sentences and the audiences.
Draw a line from the sentence to its matching audience.
Share your answers with a partner.

Sentences	Audience
1. Well, I didn't think the dog would really eat my homework.	a waitress
2. I wish I could sing.	a teacher
3. I'd be happy to loan my tools to you.	your neighbor
4. You are getting hair all over the furniture.	a celebrity
5. Can I keep my books in your desk? I spilled juice in mine.	a friend
6. How did the chef make that dessert? It was great.	your pet

Choose one sentence. Draw a picture that includes the audience. Share your picture with a friend.

Assessment

Write a sentence that matches the scene.
Remember to use the right voice for the audience.

1. Tell your mom you finished folding the clothes.

_____

_____

Tell your friend you finished folding the clothes.

_____

_____

2. Tell your principal you won't ever write in a textbook again.

_____

_____

Tell your friend you won't ever write in a textbook again.

_____

_____

3. Tell your dog that his lunch is ready to eat.

_____

_____

Tell your sick parent that lunch is ready to eat.

_____

_____

4. Ask your neighbor for a cup of sugar.

_____

_____

5. Ask your little sister for a cup of sugar.

_____

_____

Overview   Adjectives

Directions and Sample Answers for Activity Pages

Day 1	See "Provide a Real-World Example" below.
Day 2	Read the title and directions aloud. Invite students to read the sentences. Then ask them to illustrate what the sentences tell them. Have students share illustrations with a partner. For extra credit, ask students to write a descriptive sentence and have a partner illustrate it.
Day 3	Read the title and directions aloud. Invite students to read the sentences. Then ask students to revise the sentences by including adjectives and changing words if they choose. Remind students that they want to write sentences that help their readers see the images described. Have students share revised sentences with a partner.
Day 4	Read the title and directions aloud. Have students talk about the illustrations with a partner. Then ask students to choose two adjectives describing each illustration and write them on the line provided. Have students share their adjectives with a partner. Finally, have students choose one illustration and write a sentence using their adjective choices. Remind students that they want to write sentences that help their readers see the images described.
Day 5	Read the directions aloud. Allow time for students to complete the first task. (Possible answers: **1.** glass; **2.** enormous; **3.** two-hundred and fifty). Next, have students complete the second task. Afterward, meet individually with students. Discuss their results. Use their responses to plan further instruction.

Provide a Real-World Example

◆ **Say:** *Authors want their readers to understand, see, and feel what they write. Using adjectives helps to describe people, places, events, and ideas. They can enhance specific details and help explain what type/kind, how many, the size, and the shape.*

◆ Hand out the Day 1 activity page. **Say:** *This chart helps us understand how adjectives describe different things.* Review the chart with students.

◆ **Say:** *Look at the sentences. Do these sentences help us see the new truck? No. They simply state that a new truck was bought and that it was neat. The facts are true, but not very interesting to read. By adding a few adjectives and changing a few words, I can make the sentences more interesting to read and help my readers see the new truck more clearly.*

◆ Write the following revised sentences on the board: *My dad bought a new four-door, bright red truck. The seats are made of soft, gray material.*
Say: *Now look at the sentences. What words did I add? How do these affect what you think about the new truck? What do you see when you read these sentences?* Allow time for student responses.

Adjective Examples

Adjectives Describe	Examples
how someone or something looks, feels, smells, tastes, or sounds	clean, smooth, smelly, sour, bumpy, sad, upset, tiny, curved, pink, loud, new
what kind	important, alive, dead, clever, sneaky
how many	several, few, ten

 Name ______________________________

Adjectives

Draw a truck. Then rewrite the sentences below to include adjectives.

We bought a new truck. It was neat.

____

____

Adjective Examples

Adjectives Describe	Examples
how someone or something looks, feels, smells, tastes, or sounds	
what type	
how many	

 Unit 12 • Everyday Writing Intervention Activities Grade 4 • ©2011 Newmark Learning, LLC

Picture This

Read the sentences. Under each sentence, draw a picture of what the sentence tells you.

1. Our garden was full of dried-out flowers.

2. We had steamy stew for supper last night.

3. Tall grass grew up around the fences.

Write a descriptive sentence on the lines provided. Share your sentence with a partner. Have your partner draw a picture that illustrates the sentence.

_____

_____

Name _____

Using Adjectives

**Read the sentences. Revise the sentences by including two adjectives.
Share your revised sentences with a partner.**

1. The house was painted.

_____

_____

_____

2. The pool was full of water.

_____

_____

_____

3. I got mud on my jeans.

_____

_____

_____

Name _____

Describing Objects

**Look at the illustrations. Talk about them with a partner.
Then choose two adjectives that describe each illustration
and write them on the line. Share your adjectives with your partner.**

_____

_____

_____

**Choose two illustrations and write a sentence about each using
your adjective choices. Share your sentences with your partner.**

_____

_____

Assessment

Read the following sentences. Make changes by adding one adjective to each sentence.

1. My little sister broke my mother's _____ vase.

2. Alan knocked the ball out of the _____ baseball park.

3. We have cable TV with _____ different channels.

Look at the illustration. Write a descriptive sentence using at least two adjectives.

_____

_____

Overview   Adverbs

Directions and Sample Answers for Activity Pages

Day 1	See "Provide a Real-World Example" below.
Day 2	Read the title and directions aloud. Have students review the adverb chart and read the sentences. Ask them to fill in the blanks with a specific type of adverb. Have students share their sentences with a partner. (Possible answers: **1.** carefully; **2.** soon; **3.** down; **4.** gently; **5.** yesterday; **6.** there) Have students choose one sentence and rewrite it using new adverbs.
Day 3	Read the title and directions aloud. Have students talk about the illustrations with a partner. Ask students to choose an **-ly** adverb from the adverb chart that describes each illustration and write it on the line. Finally, have students choose two illustrations and write a sentence that includes their adverb choice. (Possible answers: **1.** softly; **2.** lazily; **3.** smoothly; **4.** loudly)
Day 4	Read the title and directions aloud. Have students read the short story. Ask students to revise the sentences by including adverbs from the word bank. Have students share the revised story with a partner. (Possible answers: **1.** carefully; **2.** up, down, soon; **3.** quickly; **4.** before, smoothly, next; **5.** now; **6.** outside; **7.** finally, later, unfortunately; **8.** tomorrow)
Day 5	Read the directions aloud. Allow time for students to complete the first task. (Answers: **1.** slowly; **2.** sometimes; **3.** downstairs) Next, have students complete the second task. (Possible answer: Yesterday, I carefully chopped limbs from the dead tree.) Meet individually with students. Discuss their results. Use their responses to plan further instruction.

Provide a Real-World Example

◆ Hand out the Day 1 activity page. **Say:** *Authors want their words to be interesting. Using adverbs is one way to do this. Adverbs tell more about verbs, adjectives, and other adverbs. They explain how, when, and where something happens. Look at the chart on your handout and let's talk about the different kinds of adverbs.* Discuss the three different kinds of adverbs and examples for each kind.

◆ **Say:** *Now let's use the different types of adverbs to add life to the sentence: I cleaned the house. This sentence doesn't tell much about me cleaning the house. I think I can add adverbs to this sentence. The adverbs will give the reader more information. First, I'll tell how I cleaned the house. Maybe I wanted to get the job done quickly. Quickly tells how I cleaned. Most adverbs that tell how end in -ly.*

◆ **Say:** *Adverbs also tell when things happen and where. I'll tell when I cleaned the house. I did it today. What part of the house did I clean? I cleaned upstairs.*

◆ **Say:** *See how adverbs give more information? Now look at the underlined adverbs. What adverbs would you choose to tell how, when, and where? With a partner, look at the adverb chart. Decide which adverbs you might use.* Allow time for student responses.

Using Adverbs

I <u>quickly</u> cleaned the house.

<u>Today</u> I quickly cleaned the house.

Today I quickly cleaned <u>upstairs</u> in the house.

Name _____

Adverbs

Rewrite the sentence to include adverbs.

I cleaned the house.

_____

_____

_____

_____

_____

_____

Adverb Examples

how	when	where
carefully, slowly, softly, quickly, smoothly, quickly, quietly, easily, loudly, lazily	later, next, now, soon, already, today, yesterday, tomorrow, last	here, there, underground, up, upstairs, down, downstairs, in, out

  Unit 13 • Everyday Writing Intervention Activities Grade 4 • ©2011 Newmark Learning, LLC

Using Adverbs

**Review the Adverb Examples chart from Day 1.
Now read the sentences. Fill in the blanks with the
specific type of adverb. Do not use the same adverb
more than once. Share your sentences with a partner.**

1. I _____ made my bed. (how adverb)

2. The doctor will call _____ and tell me if I need to see her. (when adverb)

3. I can't climb _____. I'm not wearing the right shoes. (where adverb)

4. My cat _____ sat in my lap. (how adverb)

5. _____ my mom told me that I couldn't go to the movies. (when adverb)

6. I think the cave is over _____. (where adverb)

**Choose one sentence and rewrite it using other adverbs.
How many different adverbs can you use?**

_____

_____

_____

_____

-ly Adverbs

Look at the pictures. Talk about them with a partner.
Choose an -ly word from the Adverbs Examples chart that
describes each picture. Write the adverb on the line.
Do not use the same adverb more than once.

1.

_____

2.

_____

3.

_____

4.

_____

Choose two pictures and write a sentence for each one.
Be sure to include your adverb. Share your sentences with your partner.

_____

_____

_____

You Mean We Missed It?

Read the short story. Revise the story by including adverbs from the word bank. Share your story with a partner.

down	before	outside	later	unfortunately	next	carefully
smoothly	up	finally	now	quickly	soon	tomorrow

1. Dan and his family were driving in the car, _____ looking for the Hoe-Down Rodeo.

   "I can't wait to see the bull riding," exclaimed Dan. "Hurry up, Dad, so we don't miss a thing."

2. They drove _____ mountains and _____ valleys, and they still couldn't find it. Lunchtime was coming _____, and everyone was getting hungry.

   "Hey, Dad," said Dan, "I'm hungry. Can we stop and eat?"

   "Not a bad idea," replied Dad.

3. The family stopped at a roadside park and _____ set up lunch.

4. Mom passed out bread, peanut butter, and jelly. _____ long, Dan had the peanut butter and he _____ spread a thick layer on his bread. _____ came the jelly.

5. "Can someone pass the jelly _____?" asked Dan.

6. "OK, Grumpy. I know you're hungry, but stay calm," said Mom. "Let's enjoy eating _____ in the fresh air."

7. _____, the family finished eating, and they repacked the car. Fifteen minutes _____, Dan's family found the rodeo. _____, they had missed the day's events.

8. "You mean we missed the bull riding because of peanut butter?" exclaimed Dan. "_____ can only be butter . . . I mean better."

Name _____

Assessment

Read the sentences. Then choose an adverb from the word bank and write it on the line.

downstairs	slowly	sometimes

1. Our computer works _____. (how adverb)

2. _____, it doesn't work at all. (when adverb)

3. We decided to move it _____ (where adverb)

Read the sentence. Revise the sentence to include a how and when adverb. Use the Adverb Examples chart if necessary.

I chopped limbs from the dead tree.

_____

_____

Overview Strong Verbs

Directions and Sample Answers for Activity Pages

Day 1	See "Provide a Real-World Example" below.
Day 2	Read the title and directions aloud. With a partner, invite students to read the sentence pairs. Have students act out sentence pairs and decide which sentence contains the strong verb. Have students circle the sentence containing the strong verb. (Answers: **1.** nodded; **2.** ordered; **3.** greeted; **4.** shattered) Have pairs choose one strong verb sentence to act out during whole-class time. Have the class identify which sentence the pair acts out.
Day 3	Read the title and directions aloud. Invite students to read the words in the word bank and the sentences. Have students choose the strong verb that completes the sentence and write it on the line provided. Finally, have students choose two leftover verbs and use them in dialogue sentences. (Possible answers: **1.** cried; **2.** ordered; **3.** responded; **4.** chimed; **5.** chuckled—Note: Other answer choices are acceptable.)
Day 4	Read the title and directions aloud. Invite students to read the words in each column. Then ask students to draw a line from the weak verb to its matching strong verb. Have students choose two strong verbs and use each in a sentence. (Answers: laugh—giggle; ask—demand; gather—collect; fight—struggle; seem—appear; talk—discuss; give—supply; show—reveal)
Day 5	Read the directions aloud. Allow time for students to complete the first task. (Answers: **1.** bossed; **2.** discussed; **3.** whispered) Next, have students complete the second task. (Answers: **4.** demanded; **5.** struggled; **6.** collected) Afterward, meet individually with students. Discuss their results. Use their responses to plan further instruction.

Provide a Real-World Example

◆ Hand out the Day 1 activity page. **Say:** *The English language is filled with action words. Action words are called verbs. When we write, we want to use the verb that best describes what is happening. The best verb helps the reader "see" what is happening. Look at the sentence. There is nothing wrong with the word **fell**, but it is a common word. Another word might better describe what happened to the boy. Watch as I rewrite the sentence.*

◆ Write the following revised sentence on the board: *My little brother tumbled off the bed.* Underline **tumbled**. (If time allows, have a student act out the difference between **fell** and **tumbled**.)

◆ **Ask:** *Have you ever fallen out of bed? It doesn't really look like falling. Does it? It looks more like tumbling. The word **tumble** gives the reader a better idea of what the little boy looked like. Verbs like **tumble** are called strong verbs because they create a picture in the reader's mind.* Repeat the process with the remaining sentences.

◆ **Say:** *Remember strong verbs really show readers what is happening. Use strong verbs when you write.*

Strong Verbs

Rewrite the sentences to include strong verbs.

My little brother fell off the bed.

_____

_____

I pulled weeds all afternoon.

_____

_____

The group walked through thick grass and weeds.

_____

_____

My mom made a cake for the school fair.

_____

_____

Act It Out!

Read each sentence pair. Act out each sentence and decide which one has the strong verb in it. Circle the sentence with the strong verb.

1. John bent his head at Jeff. The answer was yes.

John nodded his head at Jeff. The answer was yes.

2. My mother ordered me to climb off the roof.

My mother told me to climb off the roof.

3. The nurse met us at the door.

The nurse greeted us at the door.

4. My little brother broke his toy when he fell.

My little brother shattered his toy when he fell.

Choose one strong verb sentence and act it out for the class. Have the class identify which sentence you chose.

"Said" and "Ask" Verbs

**There are many ways to say "said" and "asked." Read the
dialogue sentences. Choose a word from the word bank to
complete each sentence. (Some words will be left over.)
Share your revised dialogue sentences with a partner.**

chimed	ordered	responded	replied	chuckled
bragged	cried	laughed	answered	

1. "Help! Help! It's a conspiracy! My gold is gone. Everything I've ever
owned is lost," the old man _____ out.

2. "Take that broom and get to sweeping," _____ Aunt Jane.

3. "You can do this," John's mother insisted. "I'm not so sure," John
_____.

4. "Does anyone have an extra pencil?" the teacher asked. "No,"
_____ the class.

5. "That was the funniest thing I've ever seen," _____ Joan.

**Choose two leftover verbs. Write dialogue sentences for
both verbs. Share your new sentences with a partner.**

_____

_____

_____

Verb Match-Up

**Read each column. Draw a line from the weak verb
to its matching strong verb. Use a dictionary if needed.**

Weak Verbs

laugh	reveal
ask	collect
gather	appear
fight	discuss
seem	supply
talk	struggle
give	giggle
show	demand

**Choose two strong verbs. Write a sentence for each verb.
Share your new sentences with a partner.**

_____

_____

_____

Assessment

Complete the activities using the words in the word bank.

bossed	collected	discussed
struggled	demanded	whispered

Read the sentences.

1. "Take out the trash," _____ my big sister.

2. The student group _____ changes to recess times.

3. The girls put their heads together and _____.

Read the sentences. Replace the underlined weak verb with a strong verb from the word bank.

4. The principal <u>wanted</u> an answer from the boys.

5. The family of beavers <u>tried</u> to survive.

6. We went to the beach and <u>got</u> shells for our art project.

Overview Nouns

Directions and Sample Answers for Activity Pages

Day 1	See "Provide a Real-World Example" below.
Day 2	Read the title and directions aloud. Have students read the nouns in both columns. Ask them to draw lines matching each noun on the left side with its synonym on the right side. Have students share responses with a partner. Have them choose two nouns from the right column and use them in sentences. (Answers: form—shape; present—gift; sign—billboard; name—title; package—bundle; plan—design; answer—response; animal—creature)
Day 3	Read the title and directions aloud. Invite students to read the sentences. Ask students to choose nouns from the word bank that means the same, or about the same, as the underlined words. Have students rewrite the sentences using the new nouns. (Answers: **1.** jacket; **2.** loafers; **3.** britches; **4.** portrait; **5.** timepiece; **6.** icebox; **7.** pop; **8.** stairs)
Day 4	Read the title and directions aloud. Invite students to read the nouns in both columns. Then ask students to draw lines matching animals on the left side with their group names on the right side. Have students choose two animals and their group names and use each in a sentence. (Answers: ants—colony; geese—gaggle; oysters—bed; bees—swarm; cows—herd; crocodiles—bask; seagulls—flock; wolves—pack; fish—school)
Day 5	Read the directions aloud. Allow time for students to complete the first task. (Answers: rocks—pebbles; dirt—soil; mail—package) Next, have students complete the second task. (Answers: **1.** stool; **2.** patio; **3.** market) Afterward, meet individually with students. Discuss their results. Use their responses to plan further instruction.

Provide a Real-World Example

◆ Hand out the Day 1 activity page. Write the word **noun** on the board. **Ask:** *What is a noun?* Allow responses. **Say:** *Yes. A noun is a person, place, thing, or idea. What are some person nouns?* Allow responses. If students struggle, suggest nouns from the chart.

◆ **Say:** *Good authors want to use the noun that tells exactly what they are thinking. Let's think about how to use the best noun. Look at the first sentence. The word **race** is a great noun. When I say the word **race**, you see people running toward a finish line, but I really want to use a noun that is not so common. Another word for **race**. A synonym for **race**.*

◆ Revise sentences on the board with more specific nouns. **Say:** *Now look at the sentence. I changed **race** to **competition**. What do you think of when you hear the word **competition**?* Allow time for student responses. **Say:** ***Race** and **competition** mean almost the same thing. In this case, **competition** might be the better word to use because of what it makes the reader think about.* Repeat the process with the remaining sentences: Did you see that group of geese? (flock) I need some string for my art project. (twine) The jazz band's leader did a great job. (conductor)

Nouns

person	place	thing	idea
dad, principal, boss, neighbor	library, store, mall, movie theater	wagon, boot, lion, shark	love, peace, belief

Nouns

Complete the chart.

Nouns

person	place	thing	idea

Rewrite the sentences using different nouns.

Our school's team won the race.

_____

_____

Did you see that group of geese?

_____

_____

I need some string for my art project.

_____

_____

The jazz band's leader did a great job.

_____

_____

Noun Match

Read the nouns on both sides of the page. Draw lines matching nouns from the left side with their synonyms on the right side. Share your thoughts with a partner. Use a dictionary to define words that you do not know.

Old Noun	New Noun
form	gift
present	bundle
sign	response
name	creature
package	shape
plan	billboard
answer	title
animal	design

Choose two nouns from the right side and write a sentence for each.

_____

_____

_____

Nouns People Use

Nouns that were used a long time ago may not be used today. Nouns used in one part of the country may not be used in other parts of the country. Read the sentences. Choose nouns from the word bank that mean about the same thing as the underlined nouns. Rewrite the sentences at the bottom of the page. Share your answers with a partner.

icebox	britches	stairs	jacket
timepiece	loafers	pop	portrait

1. Get your <u>coat</u>!

2. Those <u>shoes</u> will not work for hiking in the woods.

3. I climbed a tree and tore my <u>pants</u>.

4. Your <u>picture</u> turned out well.

5. My <u>watch</u> says it's twelve o'clock.

6. Someone opened the <u>refrigerator</u> door and didn't close it.

7. I wish I had a nice, cold <u>soda</u> right now.

8. Be careful climbing the <u>steps</u>.

_____

_____

_____

_____

_____

_____

_____

_____

Animal Groups

A battery of barracudas? A dray of squirrels? Have you ever heard of these things? They are nouns that are used for animal groups. Read the list of animals on the left side of the page. Read the group names listed on the right side. Draw lines matching animals to their group names. Use a dictionary or the Internet if needed.

Animals	**Groups**
ants	pack
geese	colony
oysters	flock
bees	bed
cows	bask
crocodiles	herd
seagulls	gaggle
wolves	school
fish	swarm

Choose two animals and their group name. Write a sentence for each.

_____

_____

_____

Assessment

Read the nouns on both sides of the page. Draw lines
matching nouns from the left side to nouns on the right side.

<u>**Old Noun**</u>   <u>**New Noun**</u>

rocks   package

dirt   pebbles

mail   soil

Read the sentences. Think about the underlined noun.
Choose a noun from the word bank that means about
the same thing. Rewrite the sentences using your new noun.

patio	market	stool

1. My little sister climbed into the <u>chair</u>.

2. We left the sandy toys on the <u>porch</u>.

3. I bought groceries at the <u>store</u>.

Overview Idioms

Directions and Sample Answers for Activity Pages

Day 1	See "Provide a Real-World Example" below.
Day 2	Read the title and directions aloud. Have students read the sentences. Ask them to draw a line matching the idiom sentence on the left with its corresponding plain sentence on the right. Have students share their results with a partner. (Answers: **1.** I'm nervous while I wait.; **2.** He doesn't behave well.; **3.** The cheese is very hard.; **4.** My sister looks like my teacher.; **5.** Tell me again.; **6.** Those books are easy to find.) Ask students to choose one idiom sentence and illustrate it. Ask a partner to identify which sentence was drawn.
Day 3	Read the title and directions aloud. Have students read the sentences. Ask them to tell what each sentence really means. Have them draw a picture illustrating each sentence. (They may choose to draw the literal or figurative interpretation.) Have students share thinking and illustrations with a partner. (Possible answers: **1.** You didn't know what was going on.; **2.** That track meet made me very tired.; **3.** My little sister is difficult to handle.; **4.** My aunt used all her skills and knowledge and she still couldn't make the computer work.)
Day 4	Read the title and directions aloud. Have students read the sentences. Have them match the sentences to the idioms in the bank. Have students share their thoughts with a partner. (Answer: **1.** eats me out of house and home; **2.** has her ducks in order; **3.** everything but the kitchen sink; **4.** had a close shave) Have students choose an idiom and use it in a sentence.
Day 5	Read the directions aloud. Allow time for students to complete the first task. (Possible answers: **1.** Chairs like those are easy to find.; **2.** The dog almost caught us.) Then ask students to complete the second task. (Answers: **1.** pulled the wool over my eyes; **2.** eats me out of house and home; **3.** drives me up the wall) Afterward, meet individually with students. Discuss their results. Use their responses to plan further instruction.

Provide a Real-World Example

◆ Hand out the Day 1 activity page. **Say:** *Authors want their writing to be interesting. They want to create pictures in the minds of their readers. Using idioms is one way to do this. An idiom is a way that people talk and write. What they say isn't really what they mean. You have to know the idiom to know what the meaning really is. You are going to learn idioms in this unit. Let's read the first sentence. I think I can rewrite that sentence using an idiom. I think it will be more interesting and create a picture in the reader's mind.* Revise the sentence with these idioms:
I have cabin fever.
I'm going stir crazy.

◆ **Say:** *Now read the first sentence. I haven't really been in a cabin and I really don't have fever. Cabin fever is an idiom that means you've had to stay indoors for too long. Maybe it's been snowing or raining for days and you can't get out of your house. Maybe you've been sick for a while. Now read the second sentence. Stir crazy is another idiom that means the same thing as cabin fever. I could use either idiom and it sounds better than my first sentence. Let's look at a few other idioms.*

Idioms

stir crazy

face the music

made a bundle

talks your ear off

◆ Repeat with remaining sentences using other idiomatic expressions.
(**2.** Jack had to face the music when he got home. **3.** I made a bundle this summer just mowing yards. **4.** My sister talks your ear off.)

◆ **Say:** *Remember to use idioms when you write. They make writing a lot of fun.*

Idioms

Rewrite the sentences using idioms.

1. I think I've been in this house too long.

_____

_____

_____

_____

2. Jack will be in a lot of trouble when he gets home.

_____

_____

3. I made a lot of money this summer just mowing yards.

_____

_____

4. My sister talks a lot.

_____

_____

Idiom Match

Read the sentences on the left side of the page.
Then read the sentences on the right side of the page.
Draw a line from the idiom sentence to its meaning.
Share your results with a partner.

	<u>Idiom Sentences</u>	<u>Plain Sentences</u>

1. I'm sitting on pins and needles waiting for my test results.

                                          Those books are easy to find.

2. My little brother is rotten to the core.

                                          Tell me again.

3. This cheese is hard as nails.

                                          I'm nervous while I wait.

4. My sister is a dead ringer for my teacher.

                                          He doesn't behave well.

5. Run that by me one more time.

                                          The cheese is very hard.

6. Those books are a dime a dozen.

                                          My sister looks like my teacher.

Choose one of the idiom sentences and draw what it looks like to you. Ask a partner to choose which sentence you drew.

What Does It Really Mean?

Read the sentences. Tell what each sentence really means. Then draw a picture describing each sentence. Share your thoughts and drawings with a partner.

1. I completely <u>pulled the wool over your eyes</u>.

Has wool been pulled over someone's eyes? What does the sentence really mean?

_____

_____

2. That track meet <u>took everything out of me</u>.

Does this mean that the person's body has nothing inside it now? What does the sentence really mean?

_____

_____

3. My little sister <u>drives me up the wall</u>.

How can someone drive a person up the wall? What does the sentence really mean?

_____

_____

4. My aunt tried <u>every trick in the book</u> and she still couldn't make her computer work.

Does the aunt have a book full of tricks? What does this sentence really mean?

_____

_____

Writing with Idioms

**Read the sentences. What idiom could you use for each
sentence? Choose one from the idiom bank and write it
on the line. Share your answers with a partner.**

had a close shave	everything but the kitchen sink	has her ducks in order	eat me out of house and home

1. My son eats a lot.

_____

2. My teacher is very organized.

_____

3. My suitcase had a lot of stuff in it.

_____

4. We almost got caught sneaking out of the house.

_____

Choose one idiom from the bank and use it in a sentence.

_____

_____

Assessment

Read the sentences and look at the underlined idiom phrase. Tell what each sentence really means.

1. Chairs like those are a <u>dime a dozen</u>.

_____

_____

2. We barely got away from that dog. That was <u>a close shave</u>.

_____

_____

Read the sentences. What idiom could you use for each sentence? Choose one from the idiom bank and write it on the line.

eats me out of house and home	drives me up the wall	pulled the wool over my eyes

1. She tricked me.

_____

2. That dog eats a lot.

_____

3. My cat is difficult.

_____

Overview Similes

Directions and Sample Answers for Activity Pages

Day 1	See "Provide a Real-World Example" below.
Day 2	Read the title and directions aloud. Have students read the sentences. Ask them to tell what is being compared. Then have students explain what the sentence really means. Have them share their thinking with a partner. (Answers: **1.** dog and lamb—The dog is very careful with the baby. **2.** beach ball and pancake—The beach ball is out of air. **3.** Jenny's face and new penny—Jenny's face is very clean. **4.** directions and mud—The directions were not understandable. **5.** Tim's mind and a tack—Tim has a great memory.)
Day 3	Read the title and directions aloud. Invite students to read the sentences. Ask students to tell what is being compared. Then have students explain what the sentence really means. Have students share their thinking with a partner. (Answers: **1.** sister and dog—My sister works very hard. **2.** baseball and lead balloon—The baseball hit very hard. **3.** twins and peas—The twins are very much alike. **4.** play and watching paint dry—The play was boring. **5.** Jamie and a deer—Jamie runs very fast.)
Day 4	Read the title and directions aloud. Have students read the sentences in both columns. Ask them to draw a line matching the sentence on the left with its corresponding sentence on the right. Have students choose two sentences from the right side, tell what is being compared, and illustrate them. Have them share their thoughts and illustrations with a partner. (Answers: **1.** These shoes fit like a glove. **2.** The plant's dirt was as dry as a bone. **3.** Jeff moves like a snail. **4.** The house was as clean as a whistle. **5.** The baby is as light as a feather. **6.** Dan eats like a pig.)
Day 5	Read the directions aloud. Allow time for students to complete the task. (Answers: **1.** beach ball and pancake—The beach ball was out of air. **2.** Mama Kitty and lamb—Mama Kitty was careful with her kittens. **3.** game and watching paint dry—The game is boring. **4.** John and a dog—John works very hard.) Meet individually with students. Discuss their results. Use their responses to plan further instruction.

Provide a Real-World Example

◆ Hand out the Day 1 activity page. **Say:** *Good authors create pictures in the minds of their readers. Using similes is one way to do this. A simile compares two things using the words **as** or **like**. Read the first sentence on the page. I think I can rewrite that sentence using a simile using **as**. I think it will be more interesting and create a picture in the reader's mind.* Revise the sentence with the example here: *My dog is as blind as a bat.* **Say:** *Now read the sentence. I compared my dog with a bat using the word **as**. I'm still saying that my dog can't see. But now, I'm saying it in a more colorful, interesting way. We know that bats don't see well. They use sonar to move around. So now you can picture a dog bumping into things because he can't see well. He's as blind as a bat. Let's look at another simile example.*

Similes

as

like

◆ Look at the next sentence on the page: *Jan's laugh is loud.* **Say:** *This sentence says that Jan has a loud laugh. But what does Jan look like when she laughs? Watch as I revise this sentence and put a simile in it.* Revise the sentence with the example: *Jan laughs like a hyena.* **Say:** *Now read the sentence. What did I compare?* Allow responses.

◆ Then have students create their own similes using **like** or **as**.

Name _____

Similes

Rewrite the sentences to include similes. Tell what is being compared. Then draw a picture showing what the sentence is telling you.

My dog cannot see well.

_____

_____

What is being compared?

_____

Jan's laugh is loud.

_____

_____

What is being compared?

_____

Picture This

Read the sentences using "as" similes. Under each sentence, tell what is being compared. Then explain what the sentence means. Share your thoughts with a partner.

1. Our dog, Nanny, is as gentle as a lamb with the baby.

What is being compared? _____

What does the sentence really mean?

_____

2. That beach ball is as flat as a pancake.

What is being compared? _____

What does the sentence really mean?

_____

3. Jenny's face was as bright as a new penny.

What is being compared? _____

What does the sentence really mean?

_____

4. Your directions were as clear as mud.

What is being compared? _____

What does the sentence really mean?

_____

5. Tim's mind is as sharp as a tack.

What is being compared? _____

What does the sentence really mean?

_____

Picture This, Too

Read the sentences using "like" similes. Under each sentence, tell what is being compared. Then explain what the sentence really means. Share your thoughts with a partner.

1. My sister works like a dog. She never rests.

What is being compared? _____

What does the sentence really mean?

_____

2. The baseball dropped on my head like a lead balloon.

What is being compared? _____

What does the sentence really mean?

_____

3. The twins are like two peas in a pod.

What is being compared? _____

What does the sentence really mean?

_____

4. This play is like watching paint dry.

What is being compared? _____

What does the sentence really mean?

_____

5. Jamie runs like a deer.

What is being compared? _____

What does the sentence really mean?

_____

Unit 17 • Everyday Writing Intervention Activities Grade 4 • ©2011 Newmark Learning, LLC

Simile Match

Read the sentences in both columns. Sentences on the left do not have similes. Sentences on the right mean the same thing but have similes. Draw a line from the sentence on the left to its matching sentence on the right.

1. These shoes fit well.

2. The plant needed water.

3. Jeff moves slowly.

4. The house was very clean.

5. The baby does not weigh very much.

6. Dan is a messy eater.

Dan eats like a pig.

The baby is as light as a feather.

These shoes fit like a glove.

Jeff moves like a snail.

The house was as clean as a whistle.

The plant's dirt was as dry as a bone.

Choose two sentences from the right side. Tell what two things are being compared. Draw pictures showing what the sentences really mean.

Assessment

Read the sentences. Under each sentence, tell what is being compared. Then tell what the sentence really means.

1. The beach ball is as flat as a pancake.

What is being compared? _____

What does the sentence mean? _____

_____

2. Mama Kitty is as gentle as a lamb with her kittens.

What is being compared? _____

What does the sentence mean? _____

_____

3. Could we please do something else?
Playing this game is like watching paint dry.

What is being compared? _____

What does the sentence mean? _____

_____

4. John works like a dog.

What is being compared? _____

What does the sentence mean? _____

_____

Overview   Metaphors

Directions and Sample Answers for Activity Pages

Day 1	See "Provide a Real-World Example" below.
Day 2	Read the title and directions aloud. Have students share their thinking with a partner. (Answers: **1.** Lisa's hair and silk—Lisa's hair was soft. **2.** Smile and ray of sunshine—His smile was bright and cheery. **3.** homework and a breeze—The homework was easy. **4.** Jane and a bird early in the morning—Jane wakes early in the morning.)
Day 3	Read the title and directions aloud. Invite students to read the sentences. Ask students to illustrate the literal interpretation of the sentence and then explain what the sentence really means. Have students share their thoughts and drawings with a partner. (Answers: **1.** The cloud is white and fluffy. **2.** My sister enjoys taking care of other people. **3.** I can't remember what happened. **4.** Her room was dark.)
Day 4	Read the title and directions aloud. Invite students to read the sentences. Then ask students to read the metaphors in the word bank. Have students match the sentences with the correct metaphor phrases. Finally, have students choose one metaphor from the bank and use it in a sentence. (Answers: **1.** white pearls; **2.** a rock; **3.** a lion; **4.** thunder) Check for **like** or **as** in the students' sentences. Remind students that metaphors do not use those words.
Day 5	Read the directions aloud. Allow time for students to complete the first task. (Answers: **1.** Jane remembers what she has learned. **2.** Ron can be easily frightened.) Then have students complete the second activity. (Answers: **1.** bone white; **2.** a baseball; **3.** a bottomless pit) Afterward, meet individually with students. Discuss their results. Use their responses to plan further instruction.

Provide a Real-World Example

- Hand out the Day 1 activity page. **Say:** *Using metaphors is another way to add imagery to your writing and compare two things. Metaphors compare two things without using **like** or **as**. Read the first sentence. I think I can rewrite that sentence using a metaphor. I think it will be more interesting and create a picture in the reader's mind.* Revise the sentence to read: *Ann was a bouncing tennis ball.*

- **Say:** *Now read the sentence. I compared Ann with a bouncing tennis ball. I'm still saying that Ann cannot sit still. But now, I'm saying it in a more colorful, interesting way. You can see Ann bouncing around the room. Can you picture it in your mind?*

- Allow time for students to draw a picture of Ann bouncing around the room. Have students share their artwork with the class. **Say:** *Let's look at another example. This sentence says that the inside of the car was very cold. But what does that look like? Watch as I revise this sentence and put a metaphor in it.* Revise the sentence to read: *The car was a refrigerator.* **Say:** *Now read the sentence. What did I compare?* Allow responses.

- Then allow time for students to write and draw their own metaphors for the sentences. Have students share their artwork with the class.

Name _____

Metaphors

Rewrite the sentences to include metaphors.
Tell what is being compared. Then draw a picture
showing what the sentence is telling you.

Ann could not sit still.

_____

_____

_____

It was so cold in the car.

_____

_____

_____

Unit 18 • Everyday Writing Intervention Activities Grade 4 • ©2011 Newmark Learning, LLC

What Does This Mean?

Read the sentences. Tell what is being compared.
Then explain what the sentence is really telling you.
Share your thoughts and drawings with a partner.

1. Lisa's hair was silk.

What is being compared? _____

What does the sentence really mean?

_____

2. His smile was a ray of sunshine.

What is being compared? _____

What does the sentence really mean?

_____

3. My homework was a breeze.

What is being compared? _____

What does the sentence really mean?

_____

4. Jane is an early bird.

What is being compared? _____

What does the sentence really mean?

_____

Picture This

Read the sentences. Draw a picture showing what the sentence sounds like to you. Then explain what the sentence really means. Share your thoughts and drawings with a partner.

Example: That boy is a pig.

The sentence really means that the boy is messy.

1. That cloud is a cotton ball.

Meaning:

_____

_____

2. My older sister is a mother hen.

Meaning:

_____

_____

3. My memory is cloudy.

Meaning:

_____

_____

4. Her bedroom was a cave.

Meaning:

_____

_____

Metaphor Match

Read the sentences. Which metaphor could you use for each sentence? Choose one from the metaphor bank and write it on the line. Share your answers with a partner.

a rock	a lion	thunder	white pearls

1. John's teeth were very clean after his dental visit.

_____

2. Our coach is a great leader.

_____

3. Ben is a good fighter in the wrestling ring.

_____

4. The cowboy's steps were loud.

_____

Choose one metaphor from the bank and use it in a sentence.

_____

_____

Assessment

Read the sentences and look at the underlined metaphor.
Tell what each sentence really means.

1. Jane's mind is a <u>sponge</u> always soaking in new things.

_____

_____

2. Ron can be a <u>frightened kitten</u> sometimes.

_____

_____

Read the sentences. What metaphor could you use
for each sentence? Choose one from the metaphor
bank and write it on the line.

> **a baseball   a bottomless pit   bone white**

1. My grandfather's hair is very white.

_____

2. The moon is white and round.

_____

3. Alan is always hungry.

_____

Overview   What Is a Sentence?

Directions and Sample Answers for Activity Pages

Day 1	See "Provide a Real-World Example" below.
Day 2	Read the title and directions aloud. Have students read each group of words. Ask them to decide if each group is a sentence fragment or a complete sentence. Have students label sentence fragments with F and complete sentences with C. Have them share answers with a partner. Ask students to choose two sentence fragments and revise them. Have them share their new sentences with a partner. (Answers: **1.** C; **2.** F; **3.** C; **4.** F; **5.** F; **6.** C; **7.** F; **8.** F)
Day 3	Read the title and directions aloud. Invite pairs of students to read each sentence fragment. Then have students revise the fragments into complete sentences. Finally, ask students to choose one new sentence and illustrate it.
Day 4	Read the title and directions aloud. Have students read the sentence fragments in both columns. Ask them to make complete sentences by drawing lines from fragments in the left column to fragments in the right column. Have students rewrite the sentences in paragraph form. Remind them to write sentences in numeric order from 1 to 7. (Answers: **1.** Kangaroos and opossums are members of the same family. **2.** Both animals are marsupials, so they have pouches. **3.** Most opossums are about as large as a cat. **4.** Kangaroos can be as big as football players. **5.** Opossums will eat almost anything. **6.** Kangaroos eat mainly grass. **7.** Both animals are interesting.)
Day 5	Read the directions aloud. Allow time for students to complete the task. (Answers: **1.** F; **2.** C; **3.** F; **4.** C) Then have students complete the second task. (Possible answers: **1.** We'll go to the mall in the morning. **2.** The needle pricked my finger and it bled.) Afterward, meet individually with students. Discuss their results. Use their responses to plan further instruction.

Provide a Real-World Example

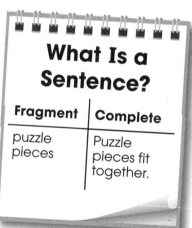

What Is a Sentence?

Fragment	Complete
puzzle pieces	Puzzle pieces fit together.

◆ Hand out the Day 1 activity page. Show students a large puzzle piece. **Ask:** *What am I holding in my hand? Yes. I'm holding a piece of a puzzle. This is a puzzle fragment. The word **fragment** means not complete, or incomplete. A complete puzzle has all the pieces fitting together in just the right way.*

◆ Write **fragment** on the board. **Say:** *I think of a puzzle when I think of sentences. Authors put words together to make a sentence, but how does an author know a sentence is complete? A sentence is a group of words that answers two questions—who or what the sentence is about and what happens in the sentence. We know that the who or what of a sentence is the noun . . . The person, place, thing, or idea. What happens in a sentence is the verb, or action.*

◆ Have a student read the words *puzzle pieces* on the board. **Say:** *I want to know if these words make a sentence. Can I answer both questions? I can answer the first question. Can I answer the second question? What happened to the puzzle pieces? It doesn't look like the words answer that question. Nothing happened to the puzzle pieces. These words make a sentence fragment. I bet I can add a verb or action to the words and turn them into a sentence.* Revise to read: *Puzzle pieces fit together.*

◆ Repeat the process with the rest of the sentence fragments. Remember to use both questions to analyze the sentence fragments and add detail. Because Amy ran at the pool (Because Amy ran at the pool, she fell down and skinned her knee.) The warm bowl of milk (My kitten drank the warm bowl of milk.) Because I was outside (Because I was outside, I missed the phone call from my mother.)

What Is a Sentence?

Rewrite the fragments to make complete sentences.

What Is a Sentence?
A sentence answers two questions: Who or what is the sentence about?   What happened in the sentence?

Puzzle pieces

_____

_____

Because Amy ran at the pool

_____

_____

The warm bowl of milk

_____

_____

Because I was outside

_____

_____

Fragment, or Not?

Read the groups of words. Put an F by words that are sentence fragments. Put a C by words that are complete sentences.
(Clue: There are five sentence fragments and three complete sentences.)
Share your answers with a partner.

☐ **1.** I burned supper.

☐ **2.** Because the car broke down on the highway.

☐ **3.** John needs to feed the cat.

☐ **4.** A burned-out lightbulb.

☐ **5.** At this time.

☐ **6.** That goat broke out of the fence again.

☐ **7.** Maggie, the mouse.

☐ **8.** Because I like peas.

Choose two fragments and revise them.
Share your new sentences with a partner.

_____

_____

Rewrite Fragments

Read the sentence fragments and revise them.
Remember to add details, capital letters, and periods.

1. when I get home

_____

_____

2. in the backyard

_____

_____

3. no one knew what

_____

_____

4. some people

_____

_____

5. around the corner

_____

_____

**Choose one sentence.
Draw a picture of the
sentence. Share your
drawing with your partner.**

Fragment to Paragraph

Read the sentence fragments in both columns. Make complete sentences by matching fragments from each column. Share your answers with a partner.

1. Kangaroos and opossums are	are about as large as a cat.
2. Both animals are marsupials, so they	will eat almost anything.
3. Most opossums	are interesting.
4. Kangaroos can be as big	mainly grass.
5. Opossums	members of the same animal family.
6. Kangaroos eat	as football players.
7. Both animals	have pouches.

Rewrite the sentences in paragraph form, then read the paragraph. Does it make sense? If your answer is no, you need to rematch sentence fragments.

_____

_____

_____

_____

_____

_____

Assessment

Read each group of words. Put an F by words that are sentence fragments. Put a C by words that are complete sentences.

☐   **1.** Because the grass is tall.

☐   **2.** I won the swimming and running races.

☐   **3.** Name on the line.

☐   **4.** The TV is broken so we have to do something else tonight.

Read the sentence fragments and revise them. Remember to add details, capital letters, and periods.

1. in the morning

_____

_____

2. pricked my finger and it bled.

_____

_____

Overview Varying Sentence Structure

Directions and Sample Answers for Activity Pages

Day 1	See "Provide a Real-World Example" below.
Day 2	Read the title and directions aloud. Tell students to be sure to add detail to each sentence as they rewrite it. Then, have students choose one sentence and illustrate it. (Possible answers: **1.** I lost my pet gerbil in the grocery store and then found him in the parking lot. **2.** Our computer broke on Sunday, so I had to buy a new one on Monday. **3.** Tom was sick with the flu, so he went to the doctor. **4.** It snowed last Thursday in northern New Jersey.)
Day 3	Read the title and directions aloud. Have students match sentence groups to the correct sentence in the bank and write it. (Answers: **1.** We got a new black and white Beta fish. **2.** I want a hot dog with mustard and relish for supper. **3.** The tall, itchy grass needs to be mowed. **4.** Great pancakes are made with blueberries and maple syrup. **5.** The mall is fun and exciting because there are lots of things to do.)
Day 4	Read the title and directions aloud. Invite students to read the sentence groups. Ask students to combine the sentences into one new sentence. If students struggle, have them review sentences from Day 3. (Possible answers: **1.** David fell out of his chair because he was being silly. **2.** Carol sang a song at school and did a great job. **3.** The boys are outside playing baseball. **4.** I don't feel well today because I have a headache and a fever.) Finally, ask students to choose one combined sentence and illustrate it.
Day 5	Read the directions aloud. Ask students to complete the task. (Possible answers: **1.** The candle on the mantle burned out after we went to bed. **2.** Our water bill was very high, so we need to cut back on how much water we use.) Have students complete the second task. (Possible answers: **1.** I painted the house green and white. **2.** The ocean water is beautiful in the golden sunlight.) Meet with each student. Discuss their results. Use their responses to plan further instruction.

Provide a Real-World Example

◆ Hand out the Day 1 activity page. **Ask:** *What is this paragraph about?* (Allow responses.) *What does this paragraph tell us about the sun? This paragraph gives good information about the sun, but it doesn't sound very interesting. What do you notice about the sentences?* (Allow responses.)

◆ **Say:** *The sentences look alike, or similar. One way that authors make their writing interesting is to change the way their sentences look. Many of these sentences start with* **it**. *I can make this paragraph more interesting three different ways. I can start sentences with different words. I can combine short sentences, and I can add details.* Point out the ways to change the sentences in the paragraph on the activity page.

◆ Model rewriting the paragraph by combining short sentence and adding details. Revise the paragraph to read: *The sun is a very interesting star. It is made of very hot gas, and it lets off a lot of heat. The sun is the source of all energy on Earth. Because of where Earth is located, the sun keeps us warm, but not too warm. People have studied the sun for thousands of years and will continue to study it in the future.*

◆ Ask students to point out what you changed and added, and why. Then ask students to rewrite the paragraph using their own varied sentence structure.

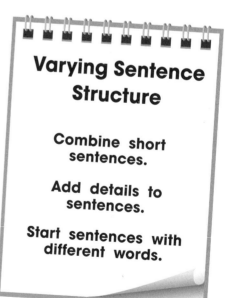

Varying Sentence Structure

Combine short sentences.

Add details to sentences.

Start sentences with different words.

Varying Sentence Structure
Rewrite the paragraph.

The sun is very interesting. It is a star. It is hot. It keeps us warm. People have studied the sun for thousands of years. We still study the sun today.

_____

_____

_____

_____

_____

_____

_____

Add Detail

Read each sentence. Read the questions after each sentence. Write a new sentence that answers both questions.

1. I lost my pet gerbil.
(Where did you lose your pet gerbil? Where did you find him?)

_____

_____

2. Our computer broke.
(When did the computer break? What did you do about it?)

_____

_____

3. Tom was sick.
(Why was Tom sick? What did Tom do because he was sick?)

_____

_____

4. It snowed. (Where did it snow? When did it snow?)

_____

_____

Choose one sentence that you have changed. Draw a picture of the sentence.

Sentence Match-Up

Read the sentence groups. Read the sentences in the bank.
Match the sentence groups to the sentence in the bank and
write it on the lines. Share your results with a partner.

I want a hot dog with mustard and relish for supper.	We got a new black and white Beta fish.	Great pancakes are made with blueberries and maple syrup.

The tall, itchy grass needs to be mowed.	The mall is fun and exciting because there are lots of things to do.

1. We got a new fish. Our fish was black and white.
Our fish was a Beta.

_____

2. I want a hot dog for supper. I like mustard. I like relish.

_____

3. The grass is tall. The grass is itchy.
The grass needs to be mowed.

_____

4. Pancakes are great. I like them with blueberries.
I like them with maple syrup.

_____

5. The mall is fun. The mall is exciting.
You can do lots of things at the mall.

_____

Choose one new combined sentence and draw a picture of it.

Combining Sentences

Read the sentences. Combine them into one sentence.

1. David fell out of his chair.
David was being silly.

_____

_____

2. Carol sang a song.
Carol sang at school.
Carol did a great job.

_____

_____

3. The boys are outside.
They are playing baseball.

_____

_____

4. I don't feel very well.
I have a headache.
I have a fever.

_____

_____

Choose one new combined sentence and draw a picture of it.

Assessment

Read each sentence. Read the questions after each sentence.
Write a new sentence that answers both questions.

1. The candle burned out.
   (Where was the candle? Why did the candle burn out?)

_____

_____

2. The bill was high.
   (Which bill was high? What did you do about it?)

_____

_____

Read the sentences. Combine them into one sentence.
Share your sentence with a partner.

1. I painted the house.
   I used green paint.
   I used white paint.

_____

_____

2. The water is beautiful.
   The ocean is beautiful.
   The sunset is golden.

_____

_____

Notes

Notes

Everyday Writing Intervention Activities Grade 4 • ©2011 Newmark Learning, LLC